SCHEDULE OF UNREST

SELECTED POEMS

I0156664

SCHEDULE

OF UNREST

JOHN WILKINSON

Selected by ALEX PESTELL

SELECTED POEMS

SALT

CROMER

PUBLISHED BY SALT
12 Norwich Road, Cromer, Norfolk NR27 0AX

Salt Publishing 2014

Printed by Berforts Information Press, United Kingdon

Typeset in Paperback 9 / 16

ISBN 978 1 907773 74 7 paperback

1 3 5 7 9 8 6 4 2

for Sara Wilkinson
1954–2012

Lover of stone, wood, metal, wool, and the lives about her

CONTENTS

Selections from sequential and serial poems, designated in the table of contents as *from* a work listed in capitals, are not continuous but should be read as groups of distinct poems.

No revisions have been made to the texts of the last previous book publication of these poems, with the exception of a minor change to 'Elementary Film' decided during the poem's translation into French, and the renaming of the poem now titled 'Table Manners'.

PREFACE

When first invited to make this selection I thought my difficulties would be largely methodological; what should I do with long poems? In the quandary this question induced, I contemplated a separation between a Selected Short Poems and a Selected Long Poems. This was no answer: poetic sequences, series and constellations still asked for individual decisions as to what could stand independently, could stand sampling, or must be considered as a whole. My way of going about writing had indulged an ambiguity now demanding to be put to such tests. Tests completed, I would select with the minimum of further deliberation, intuitively. When it came to the point however, the greatest discomfort I experienced stemmed from the nature of post-Romantic lyric poetry rather than any formal dilemma.

I suspect I may be typical of lyric poets in that at the start I wished to make kin for myself who felt I had none, and to turn misery into an accompanying song. Sometimes in the resulting poems this floated a solo voice, not my own as I recognise it, and sometimes an elaborated polyphony. Reading these poems later, the memory of misery has been more present to me than the songs; instead of poetry taking me out of myself it took me back and aback, and I failed to progress.

Despite my life's happier changes, I know that nonetheless the writer I am still reverts to the first conditions of his work, and that my songs start from the cry in the night extended into words through an exploratory oral shaping, a lament that finds and names its losses.

Often these poems have been censured as unduly intellectualised. I think that charge a mistake although an understandable one given the poems' sometimes recondite vocabulary. The poems are the reverse of 'intellectual'. A cry emerges into song, the song into language, language is weighed and attributed in its relations to the world as language must be, such being the 'intellectual' moment of a poem's emergence, and lastly, through the attentive impregnation of turned-over words, poems thicken into somatic entities of some sort, whatever sort satisfies for the time being. It is the prosodic condensation of language that such activity aspires to and whose eventuality has to be *heard* in order to be thought-through and felt. So these are not primarily poems of ideas but, if they succeed, would be experienced in the thick of them as poems of embodied thinking and feeling in progress.

There are counter-forces at work pushing against this strange amalgam of the individual and abstract, because like anyone else the writer of these poems is a social being and language is the very medium of sociability. I am struck as I review their titles by how many refer to place – to Cornwall, to the East End of London, to Birmingham, to the Gower and to the mid-West of the United States. The first review I received labelled me a 'West Country pastoralist' which was amusing, but English lyric poets can scarcely avoid being pastoralists in some way, however warped. Pastoralism in male English poets can sometimes seem like a version of longing for a mother lost or never-known, a particular inflection of the cry in the night. Selly Oak and Shoreditch have been as kind to me as Mevagissey and the Gower. The solitary poet's tendency to sublimity and abstraction in stalking the landscape and city, disintegrates (I trust) through the saving stickiness of language into a world of things that insist on being recognised as attachments – even things as threatening and consequential as sea-storms or market movements. The places of these poems therefore are multiplex rather than anchor-points.

Furthermore, although my writing is rarely impelled by political intent, it is driven time and again back into a politics which working with attention to the social nature of the medium, makes necessarily oppositional in tenor. The period of these poems' composition has been marked by continuous and grievous losses in the destruction of the post-war social democratic settlement. For much of the time I was working in the National Health Service in England and felt closely the engineered corruption of the most admired and trusted institution in British life. My poems could not be quarantined against this daily experience. More broadly, it has become obvious that democratic processes have been bought lock stock and barrel, in both Britain and the United States.

I am greatly indebted to Alex Pestell for grasping the nettles I shied from, and for editing this volume. Three quarters of the decisions are his directly, and the rest are down to the encouragement his work with the poems gave me. In addition to published work, he reviewed unpublished poems, altogether an immense task. We decided this selection should extend to my last new collection published with Salt, and therefore it stops short of *Ode at the Gate of the Gathering* (2011), *Reckitt's Blue* (2013) and magazine and internet published verse subsequent to *Down to Earth* (2008). As for the selection, I fear the long and intricate sequences which bookend *Contrivances* (2003), 'Saccades' and 'Case in Point', are poorly served by a selection; but rather than exclude them entirely, we have decided to include a sample from each. The solution for *Down to Earth* has been to invent a redaction, pulling sections from their original poems; this has been based on my practice in reading publicly from this book.

When the selection of my early poems, *Oort's Cloud*, was published in 1999 I thanked the many who supported my writing. 1999 was the year I met Maud

Ellmann again after a long separation and as a direct result of the book's publication – the best response I have received to any book. So here I add my heartfelt thanks to her.

JOHN WILKINSON

WEST

a

West-going car with

behind coffee
in a glasswalled

mark drapes across
a girder, crane twist

b

Dapple it and
fixes across

final tone sustained, some
hold twists into
the book spread, skin

c

These shades are a blue
the developer blotches on

grid skin our corporation

cloud lamina at up moon

d

Or endure the
wants obtained

watching behind the
winding up and down

e

Pushes out

a broaching a
stain blur
travelling moon a
flock of rooks down

a spread

f

West-going car with
moon

the frame steady

THE WAKING MOMENT

In summer
in country places
it's the custom yet
to fill
hearth or grate

with evergreen.

Inquisitor

do not nip it
do not blaze it
do not cut it
with that knife,

a little child
ripped from surveillance,
it was bark of
your left eye.

AN EPISODE FOR SARAH

Can you rest longer in the night with me than alone

but of course not, I'll stay, smoke rises from the
bedroom chair

so passive that money speaks, my being no more than
unemployed for the season, teaches me my shortcoming

my guarantee; I promise to pay the bearer on demand

those fields of evidence the government taps for us
of revenue, up to the hilt, we're the credit society

now, I mustn't breathe at the neither here nor there

it is neither
here nor there, my lungs disturb you by rule of, of

nature, of nature, the funny careful rhetoric that

burns a hole in my trouser pocket slung on the chair.

CHAPEL POINT

I did look up a fiction, but
a good geometry set was always
to be saved for; the workshop
lathes, fragments of perspex
and copper wire; that diction
carries its making now. If
this has been so very dense:

the great and permanent objects
get a pompous line, the king
totters away from the centre of
his kingship; stay for a last
proposition, for the minutes!

And a handful of days of last
April, then it's generally:

a tulip bough may be weightier
and aeroplanes pull a balmy
mutter behind the street one
storey down. Wave to old baby
pic-a-back, screaming in the
wicker chair at daddy's neck.

PREFACE A

Rain in the air
            not yet
lightning is hanging fire
         we sit tight
for the rain & thunder
I doubt I know one
   word of German
all the better
   to translate Celan
with   Bobby
  a few months back
was learning Spanish

The storm awaited blew
   a mile or two south
we extend it a big hand
   then it did
go on for ever I mean
       close
  like a truculently green
    bluebottle
careful of our
   afternoon's diversion

It's the common practice
    that transfer
rattling down Suez
       for a moment's thought
& coming here I dropped
       the can I carry
nothing to clear the air
 in my
   retention

LIES AND COUNTER ASSERTIONS

The dawn sky is like

God Only Knows, The Beach Boys

Like a shore in the Caribbean,
shoreline smooth, barely trans-
lucent, raising good hotels in
'vistas', the fringe of cloud,
sand fringe, the tint of burnt
umber, fading in the sea above,
refining to light blue / sil-
ver, leaping on into pellucid
sapphire blue, nothing itches
the further side, through wire-
work, *Wall Street Jnl.* report
re. investment in Puerto Rico,
eyes bored blue of the sky, it
emulates good weather, o your
pain accumulates in that blue
battery, the charge gathering

Bikini Atoll

METAMORPHOSES

The last man to believe in the Gods   He
and his wife have Fathered
a beastly race   O but surely not
No howl from their sealed lips   Their own
'containers for living'
Their own most effective
conservators of warmth   Like an attic
insulation
    Once that were towed by the
phosphorescent flood   Even the stones
knew   Stars for a living myriad
and did not therefore worship them
The stony-hearted
rise to their stars' inert gravity
    Who were broken from Parnassus
flung over the shoulders of that
reverent pair   But we who run
from the stars' violent seduction
and who change
bound in a family with beeswax   into
singing reeds

2

The telephone
set rings   From the satellite
a greeting
echoes a greeting   The ethical
dative
of great distances   Human
sentience
struggles out of moisture and
Heat   How can we
shrink from this bureaucracy
that made us   How can we be
effective on set
I do but hear the inundation with
in the body
And the mouth a blowtorch
These
individual extremes
Divided to kill their smug
human knowledge

3

We were down in the swamps of Colorado (sic)
shooting a high-priority motion picture project
Karl Marx of Highgate's 'Theory of Surplus Value'
when a steely watchfulness began to cause
the everglades unease, hairline cracks
were detected on the rock interface, in caves,
and worst of all on the concrete shield of the
major hydroelectric dam; and traces of rare earth
intensely radioactive, adhered to the generator
case; across the high sierra, pockmarks and
tumours that occupy a heroic place in frontier
mythology, took on an ungrateful aspect of mal
ignancy, their faecal sienna by all accounts
suggesting a humanly applied pigment; these
were unassailable evidence, and in three dimensions
of prehistoric presence in a district in the
modern age most exploited for commercials for
cooling beer; as at Altamira the deer's front
quarters are swollen by a natural ribcage in
the deftly adapted rock. Later, when our films
had been developed, we were pleased by a cross-
media version, far more faithful than our budget
allowed us to dare expect, and husbanding the great
experience thus gained, went ahead with the Gobi
enterprise, and box office receipts from that
gave us freedom for a grand assault on the grazing

fields of the Sahara. We were unstoppable by now
caught ourselves in an endless round of
reclamation, the most fragrant, erotic little
cities springing up wherever rejected rushes were
emptied from the trashcan, enough to make
the crematorium ashes rise, then to watch
the tender fibrils of highways buckle and crack.
Everyone wanted to star though, and every star
wanted to direct, you had to be in on it, with a
man's allotment one day a flowering paradise
the next an Arabia Deserta

4

Narcissus   Keep away from the party
It is enough to feel   Out in the woods
oppressed by The several persons
Who echo recedingly   What the soundless
Mouth of your affections   Cries out of

Narcissus   Loosening his collar
He introduced himself   Self-knowing
Under cover   Of that contraceptive I
Occurring as concept and its verbal
clothing   Instantly   The moment
I required myself to fall in love

She hurled herself forward   Hey presto
Reverts to the primeval rock   Only
The voice lives   In a dripping labyrinth
of caves   The multiple forlorn voice
Wickedly commiserates   Fills the hollow
Into

which Narcissus looks

5

The characters on boards   Resemble
Their characters   Their property no more than
Their garrulous stories   This woman who amazed
me   That boy

The accents might have me on   At any pretext
They smother the javelin
with mawkish vine   By the airvent
The leadership community   Installed in its state
Tots up the rent due
                  Rudi is treated by
their media men   To be a star
                          & no-one can be
more or less disposed   But by their intercession
Such trivial

functions were informed   By shoots of pleasure
His most intimate reflections   Issued on an out
side teleprinter

6

I'm sick to death of silly talk   Yacht
is perhaps my favourite word   I'm sorry
I have learnt
                    to pronounce it
        Pre-cog processes
vibrate against   the white molars
of our grip on the world

CRISIS OF RESOURCES

The mob dismembered the place
    With his great possession
The youngster off the floor
    Tracks a toy tank
Over the furniture
    The linctus jar
Cruel as free intercourse
    With our remainder

His early cup
    Of crinkled porcelain
A thin gold line
    A peeling transfer
I was sick at the first meal
    Ransomed by dawn
From desperate brain
    Could stockpile
Copper in my veins
    Could survive
The last electric motor

TEA IN THE ORCHARD #5

Take a moment, then assay
your accumulated fortune
a cloud of bees
drooping from the queen in your ribcage

you stand for time distracted
but double-faced

Under the hive they secrete
nutrients for winter

His name on the stone of heavenly time
reputedly amongst them

Light burns, capillaries
drain the dew pools of an unfathomed danger
you're back high on the heath
It's summer and they land again
now heedless of our bone-dry reservoirs

Would they were so
Sweat on the concave, I see
a blue vapour
in the wake of a lost opportunity
compact as paradise
trim across the shadowy mead

DISFIGUREMENT

As a foreword to science true as shall be, love illumines the ribbon of sea that flutters beneath and behind the figure of salvage, collects the suffused if so at all ocean light, to capture a moment's length in their evereliding dream-glow, its archetypes where we were subscribed under parents' eyes, where this time we haven't started, so as to be engrossed in a usual transformation. But where some time upon time we have begun I know, you have taught; what to do with the engineer on deck, and engineering works open to knowledge, knowing it I am free, was at length discharged from service.

.

'. . . a deep cut under one ear, which only the cold prevented from bleeding profusely.' Now it bleeds, now it is my heart which bleeds, now it is the ventricle expanded by the lustful root. Bleeding, it is a late spring, and suffuses through the clear lymph of negligence, frozen on the surface for many stages where its glitter was my one wish, to be read for the reason it persisted, thought a thing of its objects. Now incarnadine, it washes away the stain of heart and sex, and slops onto the page

as news from elsewhere, or the freckles the sun
of her love develops, foxing caused by impurities
in manufacture; it is one of these latter, for the
earth drinks greedily of names that become an
unpossessive care.

.

Where is my heart, I am
lifted on the ramp
Brought to the target
mark of the ground glass
The stomach a palm

You follow the heartline
there, cooking with
such flair

The bone cage, I implore
I stamp, a bull
in a china shop
And within I respire

Sliding through a cleft
from her shoulder
plates the kissing place

Within to stake my hand
withdraw a notebook
sweet as it is though true

Yet with no long words
to follow, only the short
those I can't see stop

.

Once there was naiming, and the correspondent
blade had rusted in the grass beside the house
where its wounds were inflicted, 'yea, they budded
lush and festival in the dark' those wounds
and scented letters, nailed to the wall by the
unconcerned angel, ascending and descending
in troupes; there was the breaking of bread and
it hurt and the silver train paused in the tunnel.
Alcoves by the electric track and we cower, this
one covered with soot, that one daubed in bird-
lime. What can I say, utterly? That I bent for the
knife in open air and have treasured it, that where
it was thrown as blunt I love you, I love you.

.

In that year to come you will cease to bleed, the
moon locked into its house and bristling with

defensive mystique; a fiery cube in the salt water stays to say so. Then he lances the boil on his own, his back. Will you cease then, we pass the angel for all the world as an R in the month, we are so childish. The queen's flux has stopped the warriors in their tracks, they kneel to absterge the ground, rubbing in a crater; ground however has drunk the sign. Your soft belly. The shoulders I gather, without pause. And I won't for another minute accept this story, neither the inside story I offer myself. Besides.

.

As it is none of us would or know. We lift hands against each other, purified in the. Time and again this impenetration. Deeply impressed you run across 'the empty voice that speaks' and doesn't refashion you, clear down to youth. O never to love you after a fashion, than which there is no worse; I see and write and shall between the lines, snap from ridge to ridge of the heartline on which we course. The science is there and the revealed figures, artless.

from *MAUDIE'S UMBRELLA*

CHANNEL 2 PUBLIC SERVICE

The mental frame of mind
snuggles down in a sloth
ful furry ball
drop of its body
temperature, then with a
tipped wink it raises its
That's a teaser

Don't fear it, fear
the challenge of the smorgasbord
white invisible ink
on a black sweet-&-sour

Tempting to the blanquette
the whitey smothers in
its right turn
'Oh bondage' sings the half
caste out with

The whitey strips 'you'
it suavely, black's redress

Unremembered wine on the
stove-clad
trestles of the hothouse

Waft of it and the beets &
chokes behind the sandwich
in their flat-worm, try at
least one time
dammit I'm your step-father!

CHANNEL 7

Silence in the sweet tooth
presses a mineral claim
in the palate of every ice-cream

the rights they extracted
subside into the city skyway
pinned to the sapphire protectorate

Prompted happy faces cross
the butter struts opening cans
she cries I can't believe it
at the soap powder dirigible

Am I my brother's eater
Or the thrust of certainty
from cathedrals of
luminous jellyfish on the goth

placenta of the squeezed-out sun
dipping through the blue mountain
passes of an acquiescent
so far and no more

Scarlet ladies Hellraisers
You have been gainsaid inside the

Now she's absorbed in a book

A cracked voice on the minute
shaves off the spindle
of your Instant-I station

the shearings lay a non-slip
surface on high mountain trails
from the Philippines to Sweden
Green-backed parrots & cockateels
right the balance of dabs of musk
he cries why are houses red
at initials as they always are

Should I keep entirely mum
Allow the helter of digital
alarm on the left wrist
he's a beast for the immune

perforated by it (aging)
from the straw hat pagoda (up to the)
sheltered by
what a gorgeous parasol

Swarthy men with ear-flaps
You must bone up on your grammar

Now he's buried in a peak show

Or to be riddled with

eternal populace of the body

mucus over the shadowed face

Its etching was so baldly

lines, lines, the caring rôle

we offset the sign of life
strapped on a porous tray
In orbit from the just a mite
fugitive haemoglobin or

We, and who are you to
You blackleg, gives you away
Or Thinks! as a poltergeist
the many jumping brands
piebald kittens frolic
in fortunately selling breaks

He's the director not the producer
that's the general trend
Presenting a look at coal

Stars fall on Maudie's umbrella
score it with their ear-studs
She sorties out when it rains
& the man runs with a broad grin
into the hot black noon

MOISTENED HANDS

Prospecting through the journalism
smelted out of hirelings
leaking over dials uneven ink

it's eventide the grand concession
creases on a wounded knee at weekend
these printed on its treatment not the water

taking astringent air they can
with straws in the piecework interval
where food is real and solidity
sponsored by a flank
of fittings without appliances

well they came round Tuesday we lot too

and caves hollow at pressure points
in the supine country, a clutch
tear off and overproduce

secondaries swell in the ice of determinate
history, their thirst for tropical primates
festers in experience

undeterred by a burst of radiotherapy

careering off and down the pined slope
it isn't gunfire it's the ranch Mercedes
backfires on a lump of fossil

Jack involved in a trade entente
with the Soviets, a thermal
phosphorus hiccup squirms in delegates

Pravda and *The Times* run leaders

Manufacturers of Nivea Cream, a hand and facial salve,
cause a new letter's appearance in the Arabic alphabet,
an invented equivalent for the letter 'v', introduce a sound
unknown to the phonetics

NATURAL HIEROGLYPHS

Sunshine transfer slides me over a jar
in fine-gauge insect mesh & gauntlets

sign of an immaterial substance
invalid way beyond my tawny disattire

out of my brain conceived this walnut

food for the winter's neutering, cell
of a child's voice like a pastry-cutter

quick to reply to the paged amber wax

Take that lid off
underfated

                recreant henceforward
                sung & swarmed

the late & greedy
                combs in the brass weep

darkness stiffening 30 hives she breasts

WAST HILLS

The pool is a plate of ice already exposed
to too much, overlaid with deeps, taking in
nothing that goes on if anything does
behind branches ice ropes back to quietness
snowbanks holding back concessionary earth

With thawing the world collapses like a plug
Drapes of phlegm slip off folded arms
One was born whose boils instead of eyes
were kneaded by the wind, & pinched back
The scarred ice now to melt his sovenance

Slender pickings fall to the lap of the foster-child
who chides them into their own spheres, the nuclei
of unshockable plasm, home like everything he touches
will be compèred by the memories they create before

dust settles, spawn begins to heave. Is he socially
acceptable? Does he use a knife & fork with facility?
Will he boil his underwear, when living in the world
where prompts are few? Do you rate his speech lucid?

does he spill his life-blood over a phrase, & refuse
to clear up? The quills he flurries from his spine
thread these poor facts of life, draw them out & turn
the loops separately to tap his fluid. Any capsule

of love, any midnight pearl, has had him for a unique
sponsor to its quality, concocting in his parietal
lobe a cool romance. There, for this gaunt clarity
its positive was pressed to a dilapidated back-yard

They bash their fists on the asphalt playground, as if
they could crush the stone below; soft fists splinter
A) ache, B) pale white secure, C) deep white safeline
Sparks from the mica fan into veins, & tar-thick milk

shrouds the quartz, jade, or plumps that rose-quartz
hollow under its bitumen teat. We turn through shades
but click in the small white statue smelling of milk
with human dirt, with a sweet taint. O my boat, beat

downstream in the tunnel, your pennants & gypsy décor
nosing the sedge already for cute traces of light; ray
out as emerging you leave your heart behind. Children
beat this vault with their fists, & their fists bleed

Clay when the wire slackens, sheds its velvet light
self-contained. No secret gleams out of the cleft
You take off an outside, make something of it. Take
the next outside, turn it too for the light's vessel

All the gang of your dreams rises out of the crease
you've lit, fanning with fruit beside the escalier
loaded with green pods of flesh. Your scooped shells
lie scattered & whitening, lime for the tree-roots

Your griefs will have worked the beautiful trellises
that fig has scaled; & a swag of fruit, the alien
pelf will be plumped in intimate gifts at your feet
Clay pods, they swell in your dreams' commissariat

bulging out like a thumb; or in a civic statuary made
lush as the poor transfigured lives are fed to the
moloch of sleepy entanglement. Time they shall stick
for any respite, from time that knackers the flesh

splitting off over the dunes, in the cupped light
they quaff & by which they pay homage. Their figtree
staggers with leaden fruit, & the almond chokes up
floss. Outside are these witnesses to your fashion

Doors open to the metal crash of insects, & outside
the first stain of lichen bulks on blotting-paper
Capercailzie shriek. A buzz-saw coughs. Men pull
off, in hoof-prints they leave behind them. Hounds

chew their hide loops & totter about the shithouse:
All pain is deliberate, or it will be if it isn't
tractable to daddy's smirch, watch it in the mirror
Self-absorbed we might be, yet cruelly given over

to those micro-organisms swimming through our eyes
My face is what I see. You grind me for a choice
of if to grind me. You should, you might have done
within your rights. But the musculature degenerates

cells disperse to every joint & reach the brain
The outside world convulses like a coseismic web
It's 'non-organ-specific'. Rivers start to appear
& elms to creak. Kine appear to fall at their knees

❦

Geomancers pick among these trinkets in their play-pen
tweezing inlaid pearls, setting rubies so their flush
will thud into a maisonette where women have set to
to shine their instruments; to scour the free marks off

scattering them on glass dishes, screw them in her eye
like motes that grow enveloped in the white of white
The flaw wherewith I speak shall rub them out totally
Malfunction deep in prime space, the hope I've dithered

tracks her with regret whose only self, the sand coupé
frisks outlying phantom legs, spread to await a surge
minutes before the lamp goes white at intersections
What does the earth foresee, straining colour? My heart

sinks, my face drops, you'll lose your head, this hand
in its blobby medium, fate sealed in a special ring's
pigeon-blood. Its red sea anaemone shrinks to the rock
Beads of sperm go hard on the pearly lid of a jewel-box

❦

A fat photograph
about to be cropped

where what is incidental
bloats an incident

with light or dead space
The elements

will say *Ah*
drawn close

the moles & needles
drill unpractised flesh

She dies less
for points of their

invention, solid caps
over points of entry

than a quick-to-the-jaw
reasonableness

without waste or
overlapping

idly ripping
incidental blossom off

Moths feed at this window, bury their drear heads in light
At the end of a stammer of false moves I stall with love
for a freckled neck, for a freckled ripe plum. & on I limp
to the view I semble out from plaster, putty, resin & acid

poured in a cone of scarred canvas. Moths then do a round
tapping their invoices, promptly given the world outside
within as a cyclorama. Moths tap for the least window tax
like a sugar advent turning nasty. Open that mouth of yours

The key that fastens the door turns any lock in my body
over its grooves, splitting the cylinder out into leaves
like a chestnut buds as a paralysed polyp exquisitely
racked on the empyrean, twists those nipples which ooze

neuroconductors, ripping their down of appeasement off
Mink & waterrats burrow more tiers, an unruffled surface
breaks to small festoons; the clay ridge running beside
pierced with boltholes, filigree young nettles pierce

like joints the fistful lashes behind the shed, when in
dirt one quiet & grateful, rises to embrace its sphynx
Loops lie on the brick earth floor unplayed & indistinct
The opposite lock floods in oil but squeaks compatibly

As flickerbooks of the blistered but perennial ice
creep the well-loved characters, craning out of
shadows which now parcel out his shadow's backform
for others engineering space; they get in a flap

deliberately to help their balance, their ascetic
arms retense along the tendons to meet the strain
of white eyes, whose passage herds without a blink
their sharp reflexiveness; no degrading eyelight

escapes to sully the belt so swift that it won't
turn on any account. So statues slip off the wall
& skate & doodle over the ice, chickens whom death
preens in a cool display of powderroom attitudes

taking them off, transferring them into travesties
till only death can force, only death construes
these dummies about the margin, their blank eyes
taunted in tunnel vision. It won't intimidate him

bandied with liberty through the ends & attitudes
held for his flesh as a camera to develop at once
or even before; the flash of his disenchantment
gels their dreams to a thick skin, quashes touch

Does snow or polystyrene, crisp the noise he went after
shrink so early, squat as a hindu god on palsied grass?
Such travesties now clamour aloud to have each sense
rescheduled to the stem; shadows to get their own back

in blazing offshoots, whose recanted good senses duck
beneath the rink, but leave above a backform his size
to pace a charred room, perform his ritual as allowance
He's outstripped you to the altogether, hordes of sexy

brainchildren, fleshing out the profile he's vacated
frolicking over the corpse his mouth once loved to lick
You seraphs need hands. These were his sticky thimbles
stuck in a resin tide, should've held you by the scruff

Underfoot
is concentrated, birdsong so intense
　　　　it goes unperceived, a transparent
　　　　　　roar drowns it out
　　　　　Geysers throw up stars & aeroplanes
　　　　Trees leak from mineral veins

　　　　　Hyperion to a Satyr!
　　　　The trunk no infant can do without!
　　A Seraph
　　　blushing through his clenched teeth!
A typical pander in Gethsemane, a crocus
　　splitting his bulb on a mat of needles!
　　Those seraphs *need* teeth!
They do not have six wings, the air
　　has their six wings to beat them with!
　　　　　　　　　O spiteful!
　　　　It's like a board at your back
　　　　　covered with flinch scribbles

O where is the breast I left part of my mouth on?
Where did I leave off? & when you decipher me
will you find a nothing's opposite, a mere lump
or tease a catch-all cradle from my fine twist?

No-one holds to categories. The one threatening
was the one who did, the one who faked, found
truth at the end of a false trail. The character
& the nullity both bleed with unfinished business

You put your head on the rails to hear the spot
You lift your head to the stars to switch track
Sadness shakes you through the ear you submit
to its ebbing voice, & the stars are too constant

A party's in full swing at the end of this line
but no voice talks to you in the foreground. This
is the old connection but with lips torn away
their huge head sunk on the chest in infant pain

Caught to the life, we contemplate in the sharpness of death
those like us. & ever the statue will move to our accents
biddable where the injurious light, where the patina floats
on an old sediment: ours is the mark at the lips of silence

caught to the life. Marble stains with the tears shed for it
Sperm spatters its thighs. A rose-tint colours the shoulder
we chafe reassuringly. Wrenching apart the torso, tearing
through the impacted layers of his presence, it is a corpse

with his oracle, into his mouth: it is his project for life
Here all resemblance ends in itself. Ghosts fan off his body
like cards from a shoe on the gaming table, ghosts of ivory
spill no blood, catching the careworn face which he loves

in their carrion light, now every dumb thing flocks for her
Underneath her lips still move. We who are husbands of death
slip through light with our acid tensity, we connoisseurs
who anchor the torso in an image, oracle of its own silence

Unity of consciousness stays open & shut at the box-bridge
Here the mists interfuse, provided its arches are calloused
with false destiny, where what but an echo crosses an echo
about my skull in rumours. A longitudinal slice of the brain

will show two lovers fade in porcelain light to chinoiserie
that as false origin indurates. They pass through each other
self-ravished, ghosts of a bridechamber, still they embrace
intentionally, & if the bridge they support seems perilous

of itself, it only is correct assumption. Yes a boot goes in
Yes I am in hospital, my jaw has been wired at full stretch
like a bridge the pulleys & ropes direct. Lead weights hang
from machinery far & indirect, & my boot stays in my mouth

Through stone, fossils are set. In the leafed ice, are chips
of turquoise. None of which bears a relation to that bridge
that I know of, unless it be one of identity. The harshest
lesson lies in a bridge letting any fracture run to be sure

The infant scream subsides
into a cancelled mutter:
o I am no more than a lax spring
explaining out its function

like a diseased heart
will analyze its reckless salvo
slavishly to the echo
crammed with standing waves

Racing, when the sure
& loved distance closes on it
presages in smell, of white
abandon to the last flutter

A THREAD

Rattle on where love displaces you
cannot face the dependent
world opening like a flower.

Hide your face refractively where
swallows work in all nooks
quick to dart & reach to build

with a few twigs a bit of
multi-coloured wool you'd snaggle
　hitching this line at the end

you just beg for the whole self a-
　gain to throw away for this
you will stop with no pleach.

CAJOLING

If I let myself
freely to spill,
here is a wolf
amidst forest petals

carrying a small
grey harbinger,
here is a blue woollen
empty. Its shelf.

Either it freezes
or coagulates
or sets firm.
Every sweet piece

picked up, melts.
Never think.
Never feel.
I won't give leave.

SECOND HOME

In the end I shall belch to sing.
In the end I shall choke to eat up.
Soft as a car in a choked street.

This soft hawk beats against or
nuzzles me with down that will
at the last defeat the skin.
It is set to block my mouth
with its hard inwardness: because
it is here the air I draw
gulps. After death, the pancreas
too will devour itself,
the hedge between here & there
wither like sedge under the feet
where beaters trudge:
then am I not the turn forth.

I shall fold up at the porcelain.
I shall be that much less white.
Seen in the trail of night one left.

THE COLD DAY OF LIGHT

Into the nave of feeling,
were carelessly restitched.
That was a place
singing from.

You will wear it as best
you can, solaced,
under the
opaque visor, turn.

Following your last.
Breathing your last
yet again.
Fading into total opacity.

Moaning in the corridor
gorgeous rooms lead off,
you have an answer
for everything.

Minotaur of admittance,
but you best watch:
these threads
might become you almost.

THE DAY'S RESIDUES

They said stop, trees cavort from the mirror
tree on tree. But neat as an appurtenance
they is fixed, & mimicked welt for welt
the mirror shapes up. How then to be fetched
heart felt, or else loss be made good
natured, before the left dead might howl
spotlessly? I filth. Whelping out
amidst its immemorial oaks to contradict
for a said world, dark, an irreparable mouth.

& says: names run round deriding its archaic.
The tree isn't hard enough. Its pathos is
while lilac against a spring gale, huddled
asleep: if a drawer stealthily opens
to disgorge its pap, on-disk weary
hope flicks up shining,
lit glass doors wheel & wobble off (D.A.'s
Office), acorns wobble like knotted sheets.
Fell, fell to, like a dog fell to love:

love against the person, tweaking the lights
within. We are exactly the same
entity, nothing to crow about. Spiked invoice.
How can one at all hold the lamb solvently?
Answer, but do not nestle.
            Answer, like a necessity.

YOUR EDITOR RESPONDS

Through the gallant autumn, far overhead,
brilliant dust tacked & sheared & chorused.
Light which mentions with golden nap
proclaims the flats of summer now translated.
Shadows cease to turn. They soak
into walls & pebble-dash
runs an ensign up menacingly. Day's residues
don't echo, but their spent warmth
collects from air whose blank was prescient,

prophetic, soft shapes in a drift of scurf.
Nothing will stick. By stages a parent
barrage of gauze
descends to block the after-image. What
was a believed glory, thickens until dead
settled, wrung with remorse,
draped like widow's weeds over the finish
sealed & varnished. What's given, what gives.

It is a proper outcome of selective breeding:
a wink bids to be lifelong, membranous.
Dust heaps in boneyard little mounds,
      & a ghost howl
stiffs the mouth with meat.

TAKE THIS DOWN

Over riparian fields drifts a snatch of loss.
I must give a turn to the big wheel.
                    I do not love you.

My route plan was green stick. Or was Thetys
was it, rake & wreck trace exorbitantly?
Spread-eagle of bobbing spars. This malarkey
sky-bred. How fantastic their face
smug & so delectable, blunt teeth
soften slate their scales feel. Good
heavens to sea come & squeeze darkness out,
rise & fall unloadedly: then the mouth
like a pouch goes flat for every hand's take.

SEQUEL

Under the parasol let us be.
Did. Sea licks out the cave
quivering tight in it,
whose enduring hatred gives
heart to its philanderer.
Silt of their locked clinch.
The cave in its turn feels
the sea's matrical hate,
mocking in deep chambers
silly rectitude, yet grinds
all the same to sand. O you
sullen beach, stone
inches down low to squat
lime-burning kilns, & poor
constellations, resonant
squiggles laid out matt,
burn in a feeble replica:
but still the jealous
black sands at your margin
urge into black glass,
& the white cliffs
sting the air which scrapes.
Yes everything yearns for
exchange but burns & smarts.
There acoustically opaque

are womb-events, in its
turn a silicon reflector
turns, massaging thin sky
with watching knuckles hot.
Soft cymbals clash tonously.
Brilliant as total shit
is it. Davits bruise
at high blush. Riptide
throats spring & red earth
lips the mouth, technique
to bounce any signal
tape to 32-track. Shivering
moans, chill stops, clangor
echoes the lone stack
beyond the bay, or a delayed
reaction to a hard shout.
What band: Which channel?
Under the radar scanning
sky utilities, what lurks
unspied in the stone or
earth houses, crofted into
worked then abandoned hills?

THE SPEAKING TWINS

As a dream would unwrap its angel, or the genius
springs from his lamp charged with reeking
mephitis, thrashing free of pulp-trails like

swaddling clothes or crumpled paper, so two heads
are better than one & collide each to each
Like in a stereo fit, transacting top to tail.

Bad breath would reseize the initiative, Huh,
petering out pumice sacs. Dream-switch-atrophy.
Says so-&-so 'That was me, a jerk who flapping

flew in his own face, whose angel rubs a brassy
amphora for quick profit, gallivanting slyly,
whose gartered skin as a frog would stretch

its thin hot cartouche of tarmac: Herakles of his
second nature, wrung to fruition.' Opposite spoil,
common spill. Twin heads now lean, recontort.

* * * * * * * * * * * * * * * * * * * *

Stars came over coy against the ghostly light we
blotted them out with, into the yellow-dark
integument of latex, wrinkled flat by sodium

dabbing stars like sperm droplets till their hiss
of insignificance pinned back, refaced us all
down with a black lustre, sheening to trans-

lucence under no star sailing out that curves
taut over the scrubbed snarls of shadow-fax,
roughing bone up. Around us, the Cherenkov light

ored earth with lightning, heaven was charged
yellow pitchblende. No crossfire was, polarity,
no lightning to rend starry rifts timely, nor

would either powerblock disengage. There matter
scaled its sodium ramps to entertain a thought
half & half. Nothing there with no resonance –

Drowned its weakness gave the vehement edge
to symbiotic rancour, strips that were torn
off sorrow wouldn't deny profit, tear-stained

old federals, what did their slew register mask?
Miss Otis may Regret Meaning la-di-da
repointed sure as eggs is eggs, effacement

in the style of known facts how we knew:
'You're telling me. The sky is mined & chambered,
toothed silver bits that rout the immensity

trail like a smoking bit human spoor, trail
extension, that's that. All in else is naught,
ravaging with switching gear a sky whose skinful

dumps into the bloated light of our *humanity*
at a previous shot, those quiddities already loose,
recombinant, whose sad terrestrial turns toss

out like textured soy lumps, cost is the brief
to clean up, *freedom* eats odours into its carpet.'
'Bald cynicism. How we extend to draw back!

prophetess & hermit gird blustery winds high
on bare ridges both. Down in the frost pockets,
lure of the copper wire still may cancel

IOUs written on bare skin, lamps pull faces off.
What collapses from heaven . . .' 'from your hard-
core sleeving,' 'antedates a human sprawl which

needn't tense itself to winter out this conformity –
no rubbernecking, no edge, shafts the whole
night of the possible day, it's got character

already, scrolls & fronts. Nebulous to lie in stars
nuzzle to gird you & me, faces itch with stars.
Like scabies under the sky, our fronts mill

with tics & messages, their spiralling innate
horizon: Vastness of the outer flesh. In a moment
travelling compact, logic-trap engineered,

why chicken out on one option, flesh's vagrancy?'
Seconds, hours behind them might sunset drag
unseen its slick of oils, a sharp dissenting

earth guzzle the dust down through long-shut
Krakatoas, purple insects to the far event
clatter their props. No rags of good or ill repute

left to clutch at. It was the unmistakable stuff
climbed on sodium ramps, soaked determinedly,
bade to strike forth at each's each so much,

glaring out the last star upheld by the tatters
left of its peradventure: given the chop,
shipped his pair of oars, tampering his copybook

thought nothing of loyalty to a false trail –
our local stringer might get faded over the apron
he'd deserved, but be fair, he'd stuck close

to his companion, losing bearings in a dive
nightly for a how-lit world, he did, or did
his part in monitored voice. Nothing of resonance

lifted frost, one draft, a drink he pratfell over,
lit with the darkness glowered resolute, lit
with a candid blackness, fulgent absolute light,

his soul whose wonky register, would flicker cute
regret, what else resigns the sky to earth?
where stars once were? To cap it all, earth

where shadows laddered gloss? 'Too right sunshine,
too direct, to lubricate your buccaneer old
ancestors in the lists, tuck them, tightly wad

your genetic pocketbook, fair do's. Cockney
cheer chimes with a nouveau fishing-set, braying
castigates their voice-box, more than I'm worth

marble gleams in the country park at night with
stars' hygienic tattoo Mum & Dad. Your dead
even, drawing shutters close, the less the

distance, the deeper shall look the distance,
like a backlit stage-drop.' *'Bare-face:* For you
the dark brews dreams of power & germinates

a sexual riot, brightness you tamper apart
as a whitened dog-turd on the city plaza, notifies
white's no longer *in* this month, where white

meant greed of the whole spectrum, know-nothing
knowingness. Split it apart & spade out,
trash the sky with your fork-sized *mirepoix*

of chicken-feed, the farther away they're winking,
more shallower they look, you comprehensively
dig that, consenting adultly in spatter-shot

you lust after nebulousness.' Romantic twins Who
loop your distances, some lucky hacker breaks,
will re-entwine a pedigree insider galaxy Who

knows the difference Probes only slob emptiness,
Fattened by Chaliapin, fattened by any twist-
ed astronaut, landlubber sperm which impregnates

his ergonomic capsule, twotiming, true-to-death
divorced synergy. No! Stars dab like droplets
telling insignificance pinned back. *Come again*

to a theme pub she orbits filling the night stoma,
douching the hair of a snobbish doorkeeper
with star quality. Urgently from the raw silk

lino, heaved earth & out bucked the ermine yacht,
circumnavigating the crowd with pins & beads,
picking up dross like fluff on a needle.

But holding it all together Superman in a spiral
loops the Statue of Liberty, out for the count
Rocky hasn't a word for his public, groaning

manifest in its hulk who chew on stars' remains:
'I love me for I *am* the public.' 'Don't crowd me.'
'You look at my friend I'll banjo you' 'But

membership is reserved for the *un*representable:'
Only a siren shout might beach these global
voyagers, could make our fat lips tremble

under their sleepy glaze, her Joan Collins
smeared like whad'ya know, skidding on maquillage,
on motorway ramps the newsprint in full colour

reciphering stars' colour, indeciphering slippage
hissed through acid rain blue fits of gap-
tree lamps, seminally. Sweet Buddha, sweet Rupert,

sweet Page 3, me need a hand, me need a signature.
Me bod's a bawling mess or all yours, gift-
wrapped with shiny latex. Redraw! O Rectifying

hand, justify this compact in your stack-pro-
pulsion, raising hackles/Kandahar. Flick
channels over the day-sort, alert in here-&-now

Take this envelope. Punch-drunk you see stars.
Where to be literate is shake & vac. Give
& take, give & morningtide we'll trade buffets,

fix the incommensurable. How come, how went awry
drifting so exact? Where a millisecond,
microvalve technology, where an audience clap

controls rate of output, form & content with
its new disastrous data-net? The stars curlicue
through orbit, holding stable wobbly planets,

Brookside & East Enders fine-tune her course
across the dayroom, into the dormitory & back.
Microwaves interrogate she, electromagnets

suck the semen bottled in flasks, moonbeams
gamma-treated never will die to dust. None
on board this yacht, as it cuts the international

trenches, the dateline Today at any given point,
denotes one circuit for feedback or resonance.
But you sing, sirens, twitching under the hands

of virtuoso truth-players. Yes you will rise, shining
Martyrs, who hissed & sank an infinite light-
years above the caskets, ordering my domain

prankishly, I could only act stupid against
such glamorous outrage. Let high arbitrary
mouth off, deceiving us with its cross-talk-shall,

but collude with us, still treat with the manifest
while tainting it, our secret hands-on pinch
out against the ascendant, the given-as-read:

For theirs is the too-pronounceable, contained
gone out of fist grabbing its switch of hair
locks into the chance system, chamfered

fustian over a bald patch, Lord Squit Crown:
Beneath its thumbnail scratches out a signal
satellite pulse, & the heart drives a printer

Where fine-tuned by finickers we go softly AWOL,
pinwheel belt of Orion webs a hirsute backhand
Sans Amazonian dignity, each to his own

prepaid sub, *What's yours called*. Assignments
pre-run programme Let's tune in Insider chief –
'More first calls in the balance, millions

kept on hold, stacks more saving your liquidity sir
Lord filthy silage clamps down into limbo . . .'
'Thank you Thanks I'll take anything you chuck'

on my chin, my gullet, split-screen, bang on my
kisser, access it, bright where the carmine
of one more rutilant dawn, spells inch on inch

The Verbals, Mum's the word, Fuck you, Lacoste,
Love & Hate, Fortran & Algol & CPM Basic,
Porsche & Rolex, gimletting into Marks & Sparks

Veins! chuntering into Open Loops Lovers Rock
Confecting in polyps, curveting in charged nodes,
discharged in a flashy advertising How *too much:*

never had been heresies but Index first causes,
calls passed in a dataStream to founTainhead None
calls but hears on his own frequency, Enter

'what's the big deal, who's the big cheese here?
You've got the reception. Got the repro-
duct. So what's the original sound-source? what's

yours called? You calibrate your preset to. . . . Tick
frequency? Their VDUs extinguish, little lights
they make the dark distinguished, 24-pin matrix

enactors or what? laid off or stand-off. Moniker
is Womb. Name Electrode. The name's now Nerve.
Handle's Afterbirth or what? Man-Jack wakes,

burying faces in his sleeping dear one's depth,
scrutinises peak display flicker. Prompted
by their flickering star, they shift. Motivated

brushed chrome, half-baby grooving forward
makes to fluff, your handset stepping through its
radicals, electric, neuroactive surge: *mute:*

shut into her unique cusp, gags & fits into the
rift of part-self she hinges into the rift
ironed placably as rubber spoils, resiliently,

bereft of every mark, spoiled in halfwittedness.
Half-baby rocks this sharp world's reverie
of warmth, hip to its sonic edifice, the limbic

comforter, its lithium distracter of harsh envy
diffuses so far mood-change has got ironed out.
Dear babe, whose life follows her cot-death

singing about the stapes, that tinnitus of an
Apple soundchip shakes her Panasonic arch
Stack-system pumps her hand Abort Lets fly with

Take life! Take death! The pseudo-option haunts
a rubber groundsheet, scenario dreamt in a cloud-
burst of blood, drenching its besotted lions

purr within a penumbra spilt like potash.
Blood, rise up! wailing like a siren, planets
clog like phlegm her bronchi. You devolved night!

helmeting the hair on sleepers' skulls, the day
stuck with burs & brambles breaks – It never!
it takes turn. Every one somnipotent cracks

his soothing egg, his wakefulness beside him
bears day's offspring through a consistorial stretch:
on/off: yes/no: at all the whole works spiral

blazing inside. Does it preserve the whole thing
just as it was, worn on her podgy arm, dabbed
like scent beneath a fretful lobe, servilely

the meninges fold our circumspection, stained
with imperial colours & stiff flags? The bench-
marks for speed in transfer. Don't even think of it!

agar jelly will smooth over your star breaks,
memory will bid to get up & walk. Records
play out locked, Return to archive, Unabashed

In Store, contribute to our picture of *our world*.
Meanwhile your boy skips the cracks. A wino
lurching away by foot measures the paved sill,

this painter picks her teeth between sky & earth,
whittles her prim lips apart. Asterisks
spill sodium over stars There is a green hill

at the city headline, If an engrossed star-gazer
gazes up. Ascendant to the last he knocks
on the office doors, rattles his red sabre

On-guard. If you approve what I'm saying. If you
peradventure like splint deal, steal & rip.
Say why you twisted your neck like a human

squeaks? Coming hard on a backbone, feel the
same infatuate, the same fell. Where the sec-
retary of darkness, tugged her head at the f-

irst edge that was sensible, was found in mother's
necktie, plunging from her low, kindly neck.
Semper fidelis. Good On your Roman goddess

gambolling with a distraught lien, wrestling
with her aureole. 'I hesitated till disorder
seemed so absolute it was a kind of nest, you

see chaos, once it's reached its nadir, tends to
complicated, natural as birds' instinct says.
As absence were to keep hold like a parent,

& likely invisible stars to tangle the obvious.
I sensed it immediately. Its warm heritage.
That's what I was, not *theirs* truly but marked

in the head with something like a birthmark,
Touch-sensitive switch. I fear I'm obscure.
But everything suddenly sort of curls round.'

'I believe I can read you if I switch the poles.
You see I like to get everything four-square.
At the second take, it's no good just giving up.

When you talk of the shift I abhor its sweetness.
Same time I'd find it myself if I looked,
I know. But I've chosen not to saddle myself

in that attractive breach, that strip so busily
saying, all right if you get between, reconcile
these people. But there's a worm infects,

fine it should take turn, but to strip my hedge . . .'
You high or low In your turn High/low compliance,
laddering, gripping the taut straps you rush,

one leaving her stomach below's bleeding above's
sated ears, one semaphores the launch-pad
Cancel me Then take me higher! Take me up!

Scrambling at blind earth, you tear at blind roots,
primitive sleepy eyes, She swooping over a big
Digger, filleted for sky-burial, Lurid white

token the birds Dig through passionate air to
Clash, Re-entwine. O my twinnies, twinnies,
how would it grab How would it glimmer Between

warps the Klein bottle, inside warps outside, Un-
loose not a hair, nothing to choose between
the similar, dreaming of never a stint, never a

blackness comfortably but choked on't. Humanity'
s the alternate self-same, never so complete
Opposite which opposites packet to grip

in a cannibalised topographical sheet of latex.
Twinnies, twinnies, seize the ungrammared
comet's tail It scratches the glamoured vinyl,

cross-hatches the interior, private, sealed cup.
Let opposites repel. Gravity off the shelf,
calamity, cupping to catch the stars' latence:

Name is Afterbirth. I need. I am immaculate.

Forlorn fort.

BOOT SALE

On hold at the end of a line
you who've had it coming,
Stave it on offer. In all
directions hope held out
adheres like milk threads,

sucking for juice, heartfelt,
spider & fly both.
It's so positive.
Another nest you hollow draws
its string to deliver,

adds to the great convention
seen close in a gun-grey
steel chair next to you,
Rocking smug, glossing
lenten weightlessness,

the officer on duty bound
to slake the mournful
drainage with least pressure,
fattens you for new trade
For tender, tender, tender.

A FALLING DREAM

Wharves & the high warehouses topple away
every side, you've no side whatsoever
    laddered up, to fence with;
            the last relative truth voucher
fades like a urine stamp on your bottom lip
curling to substantiate you,
    telling you off like you stand here
        for the first time, bashful.
Where then's your collateral?
   Who stands bail?
           Gulls, their convoy,
creatures flirting on your dizzily bare lap,
 teeth parting anxiously to tear them-
selves apart & together, mewing, snarling.
Oven, refrigerator,
Whats'it matter,
Stuff it where it'll go,
balance on the parting shot today's
special offer,
        on that gusty sail of skin
kicks like baby being burped,
           kite's head,
           blessed mirror.

Why it was stuck over the parapet, figured
over the perspex shield like a helmet Sucked
consumed, whacked, with swordtail clinch
snapped off, disowned towards its birth.
True rubbish doubles & ducks back heavenly
head, encephalitic with its paid sperm:
True there is no order ever cancelled
polished off, the curtains fall & fall
down to the withdrawn lap, blind as film,
despite calls to settle from that sous chef
clatters about the *batterie de cuisine* under

under a sky flecked with stucco & detritus
    after a bomb blew the parapets out,
a rubber bone filled with light
      executives, takes off,
warmer than ever where it has bounced from.
   Static fringes the expressionless
              white case
bedecked with animal hairs & fluff. Though
   bland its corporate image serves well,
though wired its wires fur,
it is 'in' the corner but never at bay,
  elseness definitely but here as yourself
            you've made it.
            Take out what you need,
            limp parsley, go out
            into the failed supply,

surge into the mains & rip
away the anti-surge device, cuddly toys
   leap out of their box below the velvet
curtains, tumbling in a mess,
            shaken out. Daft
colour for a sterile suite, salmon-pink,
               the fridge hummed
palpably at the top of the shaft,
      breathing, full of joie de vivre,
& at the bottom with brittle wires & bone
leaped on its pure spring of starting up

for the first floor, the cellar goes right
over the top, a plague mark in your armpit
smells good, your foot reminds you with
marsh gas. Under ecstasy a bowl of fruit
mocks your ardour, fishy breed consorts
encyclopaedically, a priest's beetle-brow.
Back & forth the jester prances, tempting
of the innocent Till one puts one's foot
down & up, babbles behind the raised mouth.
Shall from a high lap such a far cry
raddled with the play of lightning, flop
suffocatingly, who dreamt it up or shins
its cordage to reroute the bearing earth
with provenance, a second undropped planet

swings up to meet I'm banking on you, every
  side re-elevated, what your
hand grips, velour, what your sweat soaks,
  your chewed inner cheek
substantiates like your own nipple,
   it's alright,
you'll stay together
What's the big idea
 There's no idea, it's happened already.
Slump in the self-same boat pushed you out,
  lightermen will escort you
safely over the wrecks, neap tides disinter,
  to berth after your regular coastal run
obscurely in the dank
    bonded houses' well, cold-cast
again on *terra firma.*

STAFF OF LIFE

O permanent undersecretary, eat my weight,
way below where there is no heart echoes,
    buoy me up
        let me go:
Snap. The hollow is needier yet.

Whatever I didn't have has been removed.
The wanton emptiness has puzzled with want:
    flatten me
        knock me back
on the board like hot air lifted dough.

How can the empty think it may be filled?
How can the hollow start to conceive
    black comfort
        creaturely warmth?
Watch the in-fill, insert, priest's hole:

cover them off. They are merely historical,
only flaps over the hot blast of bowels.

THE INNER TURN

How can a plane develop into a volume?
Where does the want
            come into it?

All very well when the loved shape
presses close
          That is no hollow,
or when a hatred swells in the breast,
getting beneath the skin
            like a salient.

Arsenic mines were closed,
           their chimneys stumped,
what came to pass was processed & sent
hurriedly along banked roads,
wanted, ill-afforded, but by which
simple attenuation
          held sway by the clock.
Excess production dumped.

What turns a plane in on itself?
what flattens inside the wafer, pulps,
     & encrusts pulp with its
         cheap hoarding, narrow shave;
when it stays unburrowed, unsapped by

infantile scrabbling
    round in a sand-pit memory,
      in the quarry worked out

when disappointment has got swallowed
        after a purchase,
where the vagina & testicles
can't give their all or take in
that much, after all, tyres of fat
enclose each possible gift;
    after the impulse ossifies, after
      love which curdles, scalds
    sensibility blunted, however
these sharps of desire box bright, on
what tip where a suicide still lurks?

Where one shouts for the next course
brutally, like a paterfamilias
  never feeling full –
where after the dismal meals
        black-bagged
unfulfilment swells like rice,
   & that is your full stature –

& in the white nights nude of dream,
  linen folds on a penitence
  scarcely embossed,
      shall birth yet accelerate

out of hand, seeds that burst
sterile under the glassplate marshes,
bust angel,
     battered torso,
         moth,
implant against the impenetrable wall?

 No-one would get impressed though
down this aisle, against this gondola,
   this open-plan. Should
love engross the hollow, stall its
      lump in the throat,
   politically it would crumple,
  love was uncalled-for so.
You put it on, or take it off in folds.

Tear it apart with your bare hands.
    Iron it flat.
How could a plane
    think to become a volume?

LINES ON THE PERGAMON MUSEUM

You haven't got it in you. So what shall I need?
    One scratches it,
one trails canonical legs & arms, one
      exhibits noble all-face
delicately,
scalpel-sharp its shows of innerness
trampling those bridges, insteps & ankles
into the world of titans I must reconstruct,
      their thews bulge
anaglyptically against the void, one
vast & motherless baby shaking off its limbs,
  that impressive. Yes, for sure
                  one beat-boxes
lost kinship, vaults through noise residual
pieces totter below, & lock, & cramp,
    thinking the blue blandness
a despot getting to grips with, but never
  could encompass:
          your sinews plait you one mascot,
  tidier still be eyeletted,
boned onto your spine for preference, matter
below its so-reasonable deadweight
    goes without your thinking:

Chilled-out such nobility
besets the pantheon neglected, cordoned off in
chopped rope, hip-hop round a boneyard:
 Still I ask it with
antique, mordant smile,
First withdraw your hands from your pockets,
  don't you answer back,
don't dispute the indivisible sky
 but stand upon it.

But you brave souls whooping it over a bone
 floor, flipping it like mah-jongg
 little tablets, bothering
curators' souls, souls of college students
 pouting mouths to hush you, bent
square with backs to the bas-tumultuousness,
 eyes bent, bent shoulders

don't lurch over-far The retinas of this gorgon
 track them in peel-off strips,
torn like streamers of some guilty
 occupation force
lain beneath stone flags also.
How did the eyes' witness gimlet back occultly,
 who would be death-masked & cordoned
off, cordoned on,
 beaded onto emptiness,
eyeletted? All too many, I amongst them

couldn't take it in on mix-up, instaurate
　　the unaired pink withdrawing-room,
　the crook of my arm, divorced elbow, float:
that's where I was grown up,
　　　　that's the string
that threads me,
　amber beads broke from the wrist & scattered
across an immense floor,
lost, all lost, uncaught by imperfection, roll.
　Had a few drops spilt
of blood, of evidence from behind . . .
　　　Then what were these? What else?
　　　　　　might the ambiguous
surface smile, o given I reflected, put to
walk those jostled feet, have flung a destroyed
　crooked elbow round my neck?
　　　　　　　that was
　mine, no doubt, now which of these
　　　now punishingly draws back?
　Shaken loose in the mystique of their
airless chamber, sneaking round
clandestinely,
　　　　drained from a cheek to bursting
　　total blue, a pink vein
of remissness, the string is bare: what of the
　　rude skills but performance
　sent you footloose / footsore / puzzled out
what one you were, what one was shut up /

                    belt up / cordoned off,
        interred. He squints
at him narrowly while cyanosed What possessed
you to revive this eidolon, this One, this body
            tangled in its leaky

pipes & grilles on the boundary of dry-living-
space, plaster-of, cracked browning-of,
            plaster that proclaims
misjudgement, judgement-of
  which thread you'd pick for a wild surmise,
            flaunting your regimental flag,
    posing against the chill uncontoured roof,
cash anthology, wire runes,
            a taster kit
that importunes while waving to a reserved seat,
Just watch his end with dignity, don't think:
        Where is the pink room you happed in,
                mesmerised before the screens
    of rising damp, personally the vile
white world
                mobled up in your person?
            Futile to give anything up but
Can't you find it in yourself

recorded in a cork-lined room in
middle Europe, mouth attacked by the tubes,
making music, making a series of elseness

shipping basic tracks to a
name producer in Washington DC or Dahlen, West
Standing on the museum isle I snapped

recussions of the ghost The rimshot's harness
into their clay rank, *o won't you, you*
will help me won't you.

Won't I in my next shift see you right.
                    It isn't the figures latched
on by soot after a saturation raid,
          it is the air itself
threatens to collapse. The bland but rational
space of our deliverers,
    we might have held our own in, seized
& reckingly disposed;
                    we tore into the open plain,
sacking it in ant armies,
     worming through like tile grout, cracks of
past mastery:
What triumph! how swells each engagement!
How exactly bloated each foot-soldier's mouth!
    Stern profiles who
got clean cut, manipulate these swollen
  stuck thumbs, how delicious, laughable,
whose talk's of Pure Being, talk of Individual
              Limb Determination!

We brave souls whooping it up, our laughter
        scatters bead-like, forth it
goes in its ministry of silly walks, joyful
        shouts disorientate the
forces in their advance, ridiculously
panned away in runnels.
                And were I to let it in me
after combat,
        were I to be so bold as jam the airlock,
air rushes through my palatal pink room
                        Then squeeze me hard,
express one drop of hope
Lobing in the one foredoomed to face me,
        the unknown one & maybe the good,
One we might have acknowledged,
        one of whom we might say: *this is the one*
        the one I allowed to die
holding my breath.
        All the king's horses, all his projectors,
all his samplers, all his sequencers
couldn't have pulled him together.
                        Mouth to mouth,
but you had give your soul up.
        Cardiac massage,
but you had lent your hands to my strict wheel.
        O it couldn't
have been enough to have
        set the darkness at naught,

to be clear was then literally fatal.   You
could have known the vicious ways of the heart
　　& denied them exercise,

　　　　　Clearly it was not enough.
You could have lain paved & chiselled,
　　you could have chosen that & you did.
You could have chose your moment,

　　　　you could have planned your lying-in;
Scanning your saviour, soon you had found
him deficient & banged him up.

Answer me now, whoever lies in heavy & quick.
This answers that the pink room bleeds.
What stirs? What kicks? What

lives in the compound yet is simple?
Pink breakwaters crumble, break to be rebuilt
indefatigably. What's your fervour

against them? You race up the tramlines? Dare
attach yourself to the rock, seek
compatibility, rot your contoured nest?

Where the bluebottles hibernate, where white-
wash crashes outside & the walls weep,
do you play hopscotch, do you

dismiss to the sky the final gasp,
    creep in under the stairs amid those flywheels
scudding motionless?
Your breath was my staff of life you poked
    around with like a boy
stirring ants;
    You hadn't the augury in you,
left it for dead. The scurrying
    ants restock their nest with fragments
                Never.
Never remotely. Never close.

        And heartlessly up-to-the-minute,
the demiurge shall fling her out-
    discovered hand against the blue
  Thousands of times over:
    Taking it out on the Gods.
    Taking it out on broken creatures.
Angrily spurning their No for an answer,
    stacked in modules into a tower
of Babel up to the flaking blue, to her ossuary
  exalted, stiletto-sharp;
        Was this the rimshot I had heard
      bruising down the exit ramp,
anacamptic, but hard on its heels,
fully alert then wrench at the classical pillar?
  Huddled inside the wardrobe, dreaming
up my perfect alliance,

          bundled out of the pink room, breath
preparing my window, having imagined it
   still & clear & formal –

               What was immured in the brain
  as always, slithers off quick to replicate,
unhindered over
     chill & exact the paving, into the ear
of a statue   Virgin birth.
   I see it make sense on the monitors
   See what it's like on the ground:
You've got it in you to make me empty,
trembling still on the verge of my broadcast,
     Voiding at every orifice, how shall I
      have it in me
even yet?   Who opens before these Gods
       like their depository,
Is it the pink room yawns, but starting out
      One can say nothing,
one has said quite enough, before she speaks.

HARMOLODICS

Atom-deep in the mix shall ricochet out & splin-
tering off bass, its force out in the open
        ill-received, distractedly snows:
    Set hand to this for the sharp
        Left to weep
Though desolate, he dons obedient smiles
            which break, playing his face;
        their parchment clears the decks for rend-
ition, sounding off where the choral re-
    Shroud-knot of a cradlesong
rares sweet & musty   Now get re-choked:

            Scribbled across like a prithee
disposition, coltered off in arcs & ingots
            that from the bridge
weren't composed, Smack from a plastic dummy
        destitutes the hymn-book,
swelling cheeks were one-time pink embargo.
    Trust we in their lullaby,
            too tightly-swaddled, held
    for a token, worshipped in his cot to the nth,
but watch, attendant bonds will slump:

If our 1st contestant now would like to advance:
        Let's play, tell you what

The sidemen honk over the bar-rail, 5
whirring roses jig
through digital scanners, Rout & finish,
all's well-good
dissentience which polishes their lineaments with
master gloss on the major theme pillow
As is, sold unseen,
surmounts the earlier score-card:
Blockbusters!   Thank you:

Suffer them nailed to the door like jays Suffer
squeezed like a brownstone
Calculates their growth, keys their antics,
telling them *be one*,
be a feature of this feature:
the more you're go-it-alone
you'll stroll in the shade of gluey charts & faint
Now play Cherokee.
But only, tell you what –
Shiny bricks add up to your private

O the sweet relief: you'll feel its binding
sweat like chubby fingers,
know how breathing Sheer Class
parades through Harlem with its Selmer,
toots on a plastic horn: they'll rescue you from
fitted music,
whisk you off at your pleasure

Want to go quids-in or cruise?
You lap the same generosity
you'd wipe like chicken-juice off fingers, always.

Before you tumble helplessly, fall to.
Stanch your ears' inadmissible hoard from inside.
Touch the shiny part then eat & value
that you have.
Dare to recruit the eye, it maunders
rapt in its sight of sights.
Shove your tongue out, purulent
with tamped speech, regretted song,
dare to re-hinge it where it should rightly hang;
re-stack your plate in its self-burial,
in its informing palate with nothing to say
else.

Transmission whether software or intention-fax
rice & peas
shall be a trick you will turn, ever.
Virtual reality squawks & buffets, march-
ing bands too close;
the simulated near-miss racks the sky & turns
over & out.
Supposing that the world turns
in prospect, through such self-flight,
scared of itself, yes/no, & spot
the starlings shepherded through logic gates
to an enclosure, safe:

Dive to browse on the monitors.
   Inspecting all they carry
before them, sweep across your naked eye
for their mark engraved on its rim, for security.
          What do they glean, will shed
a fanatic light on the tarmac apron;
one deliberate nudge, one hold, a skinny ladder
   scuppering tonality
         This regard will have you covered
  fetch for time & space
         Senses pause
 against no incept, pause in their blank stall:
To receive some part, some part has to recoil.

Nice to have had you, pick up your charts & go!
  This ultra-slim, this new model,
    no organs, nothing like messy innards
  has capacity to spare in soft funk!
    You can touch it, spoil yourself!
No socket to draw the spare, power distributed
& uniform –
touch the indifferent spot the system falls over.
   Yours to risk, yours to enjoy,
yours to second-guess, & should it plummet
  broken, yours to always walk free:

the lip-synch's thinning out, a thinner & thinner
  metal between these acts is micro-plated.

Come for a hiding to nowhere,
　　tumbling down the shy for your simple cue.
　　　　　　　Laughter
from the studio team
　Safely across at the lights.
Too late you'll want your mind to change,
　　　　wish that a skein of intense muscle –
No no you'll shape the mouth
　squeezing squalls out, rhythmic
　　　　　　　gasps & bolts

jolt you like in a panic attack, lays as it builds
　　Autonomic path
　　　When have you time to follow back.
　You'll wish one broke from many
once the half-smile breaks, wish a scuzzy
　　　　thumb might catch you up,
　would balance your spine & neck, it swallows
heavy & stagnant up like deep-lake gas
　wiping the receptor sites.
The chorus of approval stops in vengeful silence.
Settle now, work up the cue you've lost.
　　　　　　　Envoi:

FOR KEEPS

When the gifts stole away, when outlandish
gifts sidled back to the gift of a giver
   oblivious of what's given,
         so who claims
no forfeit, no distraint on her secret
  loan of essentials, left all unscathed,
             remains you
never until the gifts' espousal had: *Hello*
 held just intonation, opened resonance &
not one thing, there wasn't a thing she
  took back so far as she knew

though they would have it otherwise, flies
   circling, bite & sting,
militant what throngs the winter, trapped
   inside yet doesn't move,
     pernickety setting your cover
with the old seductive lines, swaying about
on stock heels – Condolences:
   your jaw drops & ear is a vessel
   Hello
   You should be ashamed

insinuates your succubus, a hot receiver
   curled against a retaining ear,

pressing to have it all, Lock,
stock & cassette, whispering *What do I need*
– would I rather she took it all back,
complete

ly repossess, but how did she ever
have it to give in the first place, what's
in the first place should have remained
   where we connected,
       neither know what passed: *What*

       these too pressing
       backward against
       unpromising ground,
       a quarrel of insects
pinning their ears back for an excitement
           stirred up, neatly choreographed.
   Bickering, asking for credit, the abject
flare for a moment like vocables
                       Melisma
stretched to breaking-point:
           Hello, I read you
smacking & sucking lips, I'll borrow these
if you don't mind:
           But the tilt of a paving-
stone on its fine gravel, chutes a crumpled
suit-man from his gift,
                   the queue running
towards any action drifts to watch,

        it never
presumes to happen, never comes to pass,
    for all that street
bevels itself, awaits a brilliant show-down.
        Motor nerves fire off to
flex the bus-stop posts
                            & the ratcheting
security blinds, blind the changing fronts,
    every summoned
witness has been primed, but independent
        mongers paint dun scales,
            cleaners ply their hands next
to an operatic set of street-scene blanks.
  Kept in the lurch, what
chair has arms for you or saint group stops.

Ostensibly intact
            Eat dirt to engross your blessings
Giving them the once-over   Must be, must
these memories still flatter you, fruit
                that glows voluptuous,
a sudden chorus shaking the hangers-on off?
Win some, lose some,
  how could you be so insensible,
                            what field
of endeavour draws from bare ruined stalls
  figures you don't want but can't spurn?

You have these winnings to chew on for life,
    their flimsiness, their glad-handing,
What resentfulness in store! Gifts brood
if unassigned to sender, unattached
    then give vent in swarms,
looking for a peg to droop from & colonise
        defenceless yards,
the grit molesting you in wads of wind
whispers – What?
           Sordid streets tilt
away, no taxi to be had Forlorn or flapping
inwardness goes on
  repeatedly, – What do I need to be rid?

       Even a wasp
or lab-bred drosophila
          charmed in its own tracks,
brushing where a donor cleans up deftly also
       then lays down, palaces
of humble wax, sepals buried in late fruit.
     Since they have occasion
by the scruff, disaffected
showers the radiance off the grid,
       scent that criss-
crosses pervasively the growing period
         keeps them on the move:
You struggle in their van, you winnow gold,

trying to draw the downdraught – how silly,
   sags in the conditional, in stooped air.
So how desperately you come to vaunt
         percentage spoil or rate of growth,
   stuffed in the first place then you
couldn't convert at will;
             in-deep this surplus
flooding, laps at vestiges as tide-posts,
        at its own.
   It's for your own good who can own,
only didn't own it gave,
   took nothing back & whole of the world
went, just went from your innards.

THE NURSERY SLOPES

Intimate, heavily-fraught clouds, let's face it,
    buried treasure, sat on my unease
the way of carbon's nap to reside in their tents.
    Shall clouds of knowing belonging, stay
surrender to their brilliance
    dangling in fine chains like a money's?
For all they become so intrusive with their coverage:
    tell us what you've been doing.

Lathered, out-of-condition, but a good distance stayer
    mounted from sheer funk, says he
Payload of my breath opaquely bobs
    behind me but it's permeable. The cloud tents
shall wrap it, shield from those harmful rays
    sent by an emperor whose settlement
strings out like pearls attacked by moths.
    Tell us what you have in mind:

shall winter sun wink off these snow-flakes, is it
    so kindly weak? Bloated under its
touch too gentle, blowsy quilts won't hesitate,
    pats of snow flop from shivering birches
overcome by the truth,
    inhibited lest they smother their own.
Don't harbour thoughts, don't speak local, don't
    revert to patois, tags & proverbs

weighing clouds' abeyance as it were my fug of words:
    Here are people still sharp,
subject to depression, stamped underfoot,
    back-ratcheting to pinch
such as hope to fleece them, a snowy nightmare
    flounce putting its wide lids over;
spring never would come then nor water would relax.
      Enough of easy comfort,

– that smear; the desolate clumps in battle formation
    grease their skids too knowingly;
snow grouts all crevices, slants to smooth
    & mitre to a dazed finish, slalom to death.
Crossed & countersuaded, high with failure
    to compel . . . Are pockets
of raised consciousness, gaseous in dusty summer,
      obliging this plain to lift?

Snow settles it? Not quite. Well-dressed men trudge
    dismally to check for contraband,
probing arseholes & earholes where a threat
    might develop from, charring roots
anfractuose, such red plush panels hide a wireless
    perfume going West.
Over the border it's more brilliant.
      Hold your tongue in either case,
talking out, you meet your tongue halfway, iterative
    'It was our best hope then'. Get shot of

marks for good conduct, shrug fur medallions,
    shake them like a banner of coal
capitulates before the light. Brooches
    jumbled up, inter-pierced, corrupted,
here they lie embedded where the plush overstates
    each with its owner's feck.

The clouds we have to recapitalise, roll out from oil-
    transparent cloth, cash inventory,
hard cash for every trinket: no,
    foiled again, the thief will establish old title.
Between us there's an implicit
    understanding, closing-in our breath's
just thick with it. Smitten on the breaking-plane,
    facets clump together, glow

& shall consume.

THE UPSTAIRS ROOM
(GOSPEL VERSION)

Neat something, neat shape, holding me & held
      hard or soft, expressing volumes
but honeycombed
  but filled with yellow stars,
          I have had enough of loitering
in the corridors, of metonymic armies
sweeping over the plateau,
  sewed things up but knocked the stuffing out
     like an oiled zip, canals, bailey bridges,
  like a felt dummy come unstitched:

  enough of marauding grey pilots
shitting like plump flies, flattening a swathe
through my pernickety ground-plan,
     more than enough I've had
of an expansionism with masking-tape,
  where only the lalling mouth, the bland face
    may succeed:
Wooden sleepers sew the outlandish up
  through birches screening off a cut-wood pile,
    a little object
buttonholes me
       What's this microphone on my lapel:

only its integrity of response
running across the rail of teeth, the teeth
which chew the cheek, so what?
So what chant the little vermin
tearing about in a frenzy, but I'm staying put,
lord of the molecule, of this pod,
biting hard so a pure
companion nipple stares out like an omphalos,
& registers, & stamps my yellow card;
loyal beneath its cut-&-dried,
flat response
resellotapes the map, locks the preset on-beam:

Uh, sort of something, kind of shapely
part that's missing but authentic, how
can the missing part of the action interrupt
the forces I deploy?
droning wildfire through the native networks,
4th column & 5th retake
puzzling over the voice from my own mouth?
Figure who consecutively
speaks out deadpan & who sorts by timbre
(voiceprint should be used to check his source)

– did I machine this steely ingot
lain across the socket?   Ask another.
What was the instrument I chose
to do my bidding?   Ask the home truth,

ask the spike that doesn't divulge but keeps
its circle close:
        I met the forces of resistance, broke for
cover as if a breach-birth,
                thought I'd got submerged
within their stockpile, but felt tangible
  for the first time,
            might do me good in the white brush;
    tipped off-track I lost my helmet,
track's corrugations couldn't uphold me always,
    wherever I stopped the plain buckled
ominously but friendly but foreign but rock:

Poor something, shape unchosen,
    honey's deep in the rock, sweet honey's
  deep in the groove & fluid thanks to the sun
Shines in general, most on its missing part:
        the baffle's pouring it out
like canyons at first blush, like *Try*
 a little respect
            auditions the audience when it erupts
  like on a podium
                freaks its *sang-froid*; the stiff
night resolves to purge its western emissaries:
    itsy-bit of a thing,
you must proclaim yourself or else the whole
front be taken out:

Neat something, neat shape, holding me & held
　　on a wind-cursed concrete plaza
groyned with water channels, punched with
rubber studs, now on my word
　I saw my stamp put there,
　　　how could you ever be touched. White
　as a nasty thorn in a chaplet
stares unblinkingly & is dusty & gives
nothing away, white as the parade ground
　　　　　　scuffed by greedy, bawling mouths.
　It is told what it appears to be,
time & again. It has been railroaded, runnelled
　　foraged for provision.
But there is wealth beneath the topsoil, honey
　under its corrugations, honey fermented
　　crude in the rock.

　　　　　Says who?
　　Where did you get that thing from?
Thingumabob I issued for & clung to, snatched
　& bit to know my predator's stuff,
　　　squalling
having to swallow it
　　　like Chronos his rejected organs
swallow it like a big boy.
　　　　　At dawn it will recombine
effortlessly as usual, gutted & drilled
　　curl in amniocentric warmth,

bask forgetfully I remember inside newly out
            missing part of the day's
decoction, long-drawn-out interior, frankly
    these are stars like frozen urine

broken free of a pink room filled with loss,
        breaking out as *A Thousand Times Yes!*
my voice proclaims, pounding the crust of wave-
    patterns, cracking its pontoon.
            Neat something, neat
                Field of the cloth of gold
sidled into, tented for my quick, I'd as soon
    crack my hard wrapping, rip
daybreak's oriflamme,
                    flush pinkish like a lychee:
        no I'll choose quartz for accuracy
as honey had not rotted, nor did mummify,
crystallizing 12,000,000 torn wings;
                white will splinter
as they upswarm, to bedazzle the aerial masses:

    ahead of their lines of attack, fall freely.

STAGES ALONG THE LICHWAY

in respect of MARK HYATT

Are they agreed,
        still tinkering round the heart,
rubbing their fingers over a notch in a blowstone;
have they reached their verdict, every bony lot
is cast & counted over –
                Is he dross or a bubble
twinkles across a narrow gorge?
            Straightening up,
they slam with a flourish tight his working parts,
no go, *pas marche:*
             The vacancy isn't available.
Don't call us, we'll contact you
          when orders pick up.

Chemical reek will blind his train of attendants,
             vista mutes
drip oil into the slough;
          & splintering
blobby chalk, the bypass shimmers with vapour.
This heather mat he was thrown on, in appearance
fumblingly got changed.
        Sat with his neck abjected,
        braced against the air.

Did he reach a decision,
didn't he buy it!
crouched up to the wall like artificial skin
                              nailed flat.

   You have lived on peelings how long?
                     In stannary
towns where dust flues on escaping warmth & turns
        & granite ticks through blowhouses,
etched sharply on the rough-hewn he starts to blur.
   Got to break
from the micro-climate, give him back a profile,
                     much-loved cheek
                     chill as a shadow,
      chill as a hand from outside
      held to the cheek,
holds the stretched hide to ransom
peg on peg,
            was it a burn off chill or smug hysteria
   dipped him into the shadows till deep mauve?
Shadows,
or was it his skin blistered when they touched?
      Bearers stir from their long ease
            to heft the oak. So previous,
this man Mark, quick to catch his bird at daybreak,
sharp to the air's compliance,
            jumps up off his bed & makes strides

rooted in the blowhouse still, still fuming, never
        shaking his wraps of shadow off,
    leaving no imprint over bracken.
                Snap-yellow the croziers curl,
    lights bend downward over his crib the satellite
courtiers circle,
            undertakes feeding the slot of future gain,
squirting 3-in-1 oil,
        worry out spikes or teething-ring.
                The tip
            of his tongue they snatch,
                wrench the lips,
fiddle the score-line faithfully kept to himself.
                Teeth won't
grind, there aren't any:

Mark speech-exiled, no recourse but gulp
his introject before a cricking, terrible shortage
        potash stains
should break to roughen his tongue.
                His caddis-worm,
                his louse,
the gibberish of familiar lies, the mimic thrush
            palavering his ears like an adviser
                he might trust,
break into an octet, a bird-bright cantata,
        break for a sour mash & sparse granite.
The shadow-hives he refills

mechanically
portion-fed from implants & his outposts,
smoke with cash prizes, sullying
supposed air,
throng the rising flue of speech, inspirited.
In purple it digressed
out like endless like unforaged clover
came up for more, yet Mark
inch by inch, how his procession servofeeds –
piped to every room, doesn't move the air:
Secretive or universal, that's your alternative!
A great gulp of air as mould for the anatomy
renewed twelve times a minute
The business, you bet, the goods!

Smelting–
chimneys, years pass, desecrate an 'original'
You're hard on the inane.
Mark like pink invective swamps the hillock
Night-following should ramp
this outcrop of his wealthiness, its signal surge
as at some squalid coup, brays
martially,
& tying him up with hashes, dumps;
briskly efficient
unpinning the rapturous air off his arms
He's playing dead, betrayed
by buds – this one's a rudimentary arm.

                    The chimney jabs
                    autistic,
                    his suppressed shout
          wrinkles the water sky in childish heats & sweat;
          he lays a fire, but to blow the downdraft
                    back's beyond his strength . . . . .
                              seriffed
          eye-tubers, caught, couldn't transgress his line:
                    Scrunch the paper, scrunch the dead bracken
                              Twist it up for a lost bet,
                    can't take a touch when the clinker's hardened
          Forget it
                    Full of his dead weight:

          Unrestingly he toiled, how could he count the pails
                    he'd lugged over this top-bar or carried
                              stooped beneath his arch,
                              Chains of one unmet need,
          chains across a surface unremitted with seams
                    clank beside their channel,
                    circling untended.
                                        Ravelling out no prospect,
          not one earthly.
                                        Shipping containers with false
          tops & sides, deposited on the landing-stage,
                    where's his private securities box?
                                        Grocery boxes
          heaped behind the check-out, hides for cats

& vagrants, printed *Unrepeatable Offer* –
evening's purple

        stomachs the retentive air,
the green rill squelches underfoot
   While seepage saturates the high meadow
cloudberries & speedwell, the air

           bubbles & throats,
could even this be packed & offered?
      As a casual say-so
   functionary affirms, wipes fastidiously,
then springtraps his conclusive avalanche of death
     A climate he's exactly set.

      & all's in, all will be
  found,
by poking through the dustbins at the maisonettes,
  the substations light rolls off in sheets
  Rummaging for a wish-bone,
poking where surviving
plants & vegetables

     have their growth stopped.
   Catch it on the skin then like melanosis,
shimmer heat like chlorophyll,

      should take in
  altogether too much till the rivets snap
across the moor root-compacted,

      locked vertebrae.
    Summer, shall it billow,

velar like a sounding-sheet
                    ridged & tented up
banks of gorse, they flaunt their popularity
inward-bound, carve
                    their way to Lydford, scuffing pollen
trudging through the gorse-buds & bramble.
                    He had money to burn, his dust
        in its bowl of metered wealth.

                                    Motes
from an aluminium packet
                    swollen in his billycan,
    bits of carrot, bits of something red, he's
got dust to commemorate & strew with a ghost hand,
            the hand they felt was a crude
        Fact, Suddenly.

                                    Shadows
against the cheek get sullied with coal-dust,
            mud
    spatters the cerements Hollowed & scooped,
        stinking gourd is the folly
candle-lit to his teeth:
    it's Halloween;
                    your own discovery
seeds under the awning,
                    monkeying in your purple frock
        Hurry to stuff your cavity with new innards.
Then reinvent those characters
                    daybreak tensely draws,

scribbled upon the slopes by cloud battalions:

    Are you ready to face dawn –

    a carrot up your arsehole

    a thumb down your throat,

what dealings did you clinch while at rest?

Comportment we shall acquire, after the dwarf oaks'

    insistence. Time hung loose,

       fat lichen

        drapes the trees,

his bearing wobbles the steps of this cortège,

   hard-copy across their inner lichway, lurching

                   down its peaty

rain-recursive track,

      till rested in its inside-out, till high

in the heart of a pink spatter

         they come to his granite yard

         They too collapse.

             Lark-spangled

air addresses him,

   catch-phrases, proverbs, piece together his

ordinariness can't take, how can it take.

           Where he had walked

drenched to the skin, dredged in the gorse pollen,

or gangled upon the mat.

          He who has nothing to him.

          Nothing inside.

          Is solid.

This box they put their hands to, gestures
thoroughly taped, sun flashing like bone
    dominoes racked the heart, blew the heart,
instate the heart where it had been budgeted for:

Then follow the familiar track,
springy turf that would lift their stumbling feet,
    mud to accept onerousness.
                              Bear his pall
purple against the cheek,
        impressions full when the air ruffles
Water wells but it's brackish, don't yet drink.
Don't imagine anything comes out fresh.
                              How
shall we stand the declivities,
    how consist on the summit
    packed like seeds in rabbit droppings
    sheeps-eyes crows have pecked:
                Now evidently the dust-motes stream
over the sky
                trepanned in pink behind we bearers
Imitating rocks' flux
Shimmering lights of Mercury & Venus.
            The trickling marsh is steeped
    layered reflections
        Every bit of our way. This was
    what he had kept to himself, shrinkingly,
pent before the day broke:

So trust the shadows.

     Remonstrate him solid.

       Holding at eyes' length

     the lichway, wheel & swoop

these his mortal remains, convolute like the gulls

    Scavenge his forgetfulness, bear fruit.

ENVOY

Mark, this is a hole, a real, unbearable hole
the workmen stuff with sound-bites & cable media,
quivering & heaving underfoot, a foul quagmire
incautiously our feet depress. It won't stash away,
but nonetheless it revolts our scutty appetites.
Since we can't eat, let's make towards the slope's
definite shadow, anchoring our figures so obtuse
as to have no sense of inner being. Delighted
we could assume the topicality of the clouds, pace
gloomily on the leash of a sudden brilliant break
thronged with buoyant seeds, highway to pollen.
Don't take it for a script, awaiting his reshuffle,
laid out for the adept's surplus. It's first base,
the shadows aren't ours; we nag them like an ache.

In the stomach, the knitted pouch, humours fight,
stripping the lambs-tail & extricating breath-yarn,

pouched in fat-mottled sky, in every whimpled
brook's resumé, which recollect; pirate a fidelity
for whom we stir & shall make redress. Firstly
not accumulate or bury, neither should we drape
thick the cloth, like song-birds engrossing space.
Subsequently parting in these shadows we entice,
but cast by their progeny. These collect in turn
lint-innerness for the belly our innerness empties.

SPREAD-EAGLE

Whoever does or did, did it down a superb
grain of Up to here
some await life, their empty
mamelon inverts,
may harden, what can quench or smoulder?

Rubbing down, they hook all they're worth
to a child's lisping
formula: sit in a chair, get old & die,
finger the stone till it
burst like a blood blister.

Straight away we must act to prevent this.
Rain's insistence draws out
over opposite hills. Rabbit-arsed,
a nailed person
clambers over a harbour wobbles emptily.

Hunger slides across hunger. Hunger melts,
over the neutral
glass to open slowly,
reft but how descry later on,
bellied, smoothing a shingle spit down.

MOOD MUSIC

Big boy, you grasp at what was inevitable.
A hot hatch tears away; & sun's pursuit
      flat-out, full-throttle
repertoire of moods, you access through
a half-incision, glares & crashes in, deep
    upholstery;
is it a recogniser, father's neck
      burns on the leathern back seat?
What about the burn in the baby-blue wool?

Snared in Playing Place, then a quick call
    secures your release.
           Click-clunk.
This is the end of what you believed
yours by birthright,
    felt you had been cut out of
gone with the seat bars for scrap, dragged
into the realm of chill hygiene.
A world in its every detail becomes lost.

Is there a trickle wanders cut through mud?

1

Not a trace. No a trace at the least would unwind,
   turning in thick air.
But this arcade breath whooshing above,
                     grandstanding
overpass, how could anyone notch
the protocols it runs through our teeth?
   Uniformly diced throughout this scam we have,
between suns the short wave bounce
throbs in binaural chaos.
   What conflict have I been tasting like a dose? –

naked sumptuousness, ripping the mask off a manu-
   facturer's tight margin /
                   Zero wait state
controls then blurs the presentation.
   Was it me or mine or both, stripped of decor,
pressed within its packet, turning
turtle as though reduced activity meant change –
   Where did I meet that hungry brute
who jackal-headed –
Forget I went the distance,
     mask inundation sups from a blue desert.
  Dying in mud with a full belly.

Lightning shan't repeat, no I,
don't let go-begging
hooks bristle for our fine stand of elms,
            for equity, for due proceeding
   shadows for them, frost
fringes over the eaves which then warmth abrades
Me or its or both, deciding before soaked earth
resolves to shut its trap. On or in it clinches.
            Adventures, yes they were real,
sash opportunities were cried bluff & up,
while one distorting rig
caught fire, one piano, one accordion, I'd hymn
   fearsome inactivity thrown upstairs,
You should have taken readings, O
discreet compiler, O familiar sort hand gets to throw
flash-floods up the wadis.
I who cut my teeth on the did-shoulder
fell back on resources I once held beneath contempt

   once chewed at them, once held light
dripping under my wing-sweep.
      That has been entered in the minutes.
            Unfeeling, moving hand,
it's your play, compile a run-time hierarchy of goals;
   hand, with a care
velcro units on our conceptual map, make them stick.
Though fierce jets of refusing scythe
through an administered world, such hands

deliver right on target, blessings onto the near bales
           which might be military
children, might be matériel,
     antagonists in spirit leave the stand littered
expensive stuff, shavings of distinction
yet to be theorised, snap at their animals' legs,
bend round to court them diplomatically; hand,
     feel free.

So? So? There was less than rumour stanch-breathed
           water filling my trap.
But could I know if trapped
through sperm's algorithm, egg compliance?
Keeping channels open to keep things the same,
     inherited but a pre-written CV
downloads to irrigate the strip, lubricate its channels.

However could distrain suck sponge? Spill on it
then wring dry; this demanded genuine courage!
                         Drummed
     onto the substitute bench,
                 still unenthralled, deciduous
atop the bucking body
     Once more a breach
shall operate on the my-voice,
                 torn-off receipt, known
to carry its flesh up-front like dead,
like motivation. Not quite what we'd envisaged,

bunkering sand on the map-table, strewn already
with spongy trees, my face would topple onto soon.

What, you ask, did I feel? I think I felt upset,
        remote to emote, no best stop,
membered, such as you are, as such pair of compasses.
I'm definitely tense
        auditor to the bones of the head
pegged together & woven to make this devil's tail.

2

The meanings muscled in on me, their cleugh urge
   thick with droppings,
                             pockmarked with
nostalgic Gatling Gun nests,
flight simulators crammed with young
                      jostling & speechifying,
    bombing their tabernacles
white.
'We have numbers against their mass'
                      wise heads say.
  How could they resist unless,
lest die back to an ageing case which flopped shut
sorrowfully, their case like trenched mud fell in.
     Let motivation thrive
between this rock & a hard place.
 Part presents for parcel
         which unpacked,
hooks into the free
radicals across the spectrum,
                 hostages on this channel
wheedled out from white rubbish
       Stuck, unstuck, restuck:
Whose downcast eyes
     rain good on you, a Buddha unreconciled
to what he emits,
jostled by magnetic fields, rearranged

for maximum throughput, for fresher-field bombing, dumped

overproduction, dumped fire.
                    A gross of slick concern
well-mashed, beaten thin to hang like watered silk
    deflects desert blink;
        How come, came no-one would shout?
Nor adults engorge. Occupying
cellular days, britched off by the raster
            voice whose hooks & summonses, re-skew
occupant nerves
strain from desert shield to a wet run,
    The world's working version here comes close.
The complete package refolds as the True Offensive.
        Cross-abuts, packs a revetment hard,
                time to break the bridge
To dominate the waves on platforms of hard oil.
Received not related.
Saying <It is I> to scatter.
                Scattering to East & North,
holding my slip heart
against its timing module, flash from pier to pier!

Now all stay flop without feeling, sandbank-entities,
    stripping them of flowery banks
            Even stop the boulder, wearing away
sensational blood.

It imitates love but without echo
crossing between the riders, reservations, due cause.
                    You stamp, Stay Put
shall work the change.
                Scenario jump cut.
Jumpworld shall seize the Heights
            Jump fingers work at the Strip
where before was nothing but monocle stray mush,

            radio shades disoccupy
Tehran to Algiers, clusters, armed militias
crackle for that old command economy. Right,
I'll take one more call. Fear prickles, ready-bled cup.
                Some do in-service Do
response to specific conditions
        Rub-down passes
clattering with half-heard calls to prayer
                        stalk European jazz;
            finesse, obtrusive stealth
muddies the way through (there, one has to
take it as a stand of elms breathes, there, one has
to predict the tender wings) –
                And the cloud insinuative,
an interloper backing out, prophecies
for all the world its own source as Future –
keeping supply lines clear, lines of increase flash up

making away with someone else's top score,
        calculates the pass
mapped already for its big link to cable,
one-way cable
        phylogenic at least like these birth-remains,
remains no longer sand-choked but then
                                brutally occupied?
    The lock on the subdirectory tree
bores home.
Bethesda newly, heaping belligerent mud on a map,
licking it in dollops, That was me
        grinning, combative,
finally locked on to re-tank,
delivers this beautiful packet of change.
                        Watch as I charge
    oxygen suck, squirt, genial slaughter.
This land is truly mine. I stretch fertility over,
        burning its tares & its pavilions.

OPERATIONS

To assemble the lily. Gloss half-smeared
slips like a thumbprint broken through

sweet glaze; the visible hymen flaps;
a sky funereal peels from a sloping pond

hot sun beats or mains rupture plenishes.
The confectioner's system purrs easily:

summer stripes & smash, do to construct
flaked out, the numbed inquisitor of

feeling propped their water plate. JCBs
shall batter, cars shall rend & groove

natural piety's cover, circulate in
fine fettle. Sugar gushes plentifully.

This kidney island, poor Ind, which half-
slipped on sweets unwrapped, powered

with cane trash, stayed discovery, waits
insulin now turns its sweet to plenty

turn to the clear inlet pain, filled
with Arawak ghosts people a clear glaze,

neither slave nor indentured, dead
processors of sweets wired its virginity.

Petals rattle & smart, rewire together
proof for the technician's fingering

green stairwells, green detention doors
slamming into a kelson swinging low

one after another, endless decompression,
& never a breach to break out through.

TECHNICAL SUPPORT

'Crisp leaf', the 'fresh', 'Old Nettleshanks'
logarithmically, behind join-the-points

dealt an indelible bruise where hatreds wore
out in strands of refined spermy whey,

conferred it on any sunny patch, it shows
through the deeps of satisfaction & blisters.

Canary Bill would recite a number plate,
chaos too seemed wet as out of a glass stick,

that whitlow under his thumb surely was no
hammer job, physical characteristics

backed out from the menu system, still
the operatives continue to voice feelings

anthropologically, leaving their trail dead.
Match of needs to identified resources,

tender for B, tender for C tranships
infantas for gold for arms for the simulation

stripping retrievable hurt, hanks & spleen:
But that Intelligence Johnny, he folds

up on his spatchcock manual, *Dies Irae*
fuse the teeming decks to an OHP transparency.

THE RED PALETTE

Fine detail in its red coats
    the parents went to applaud,

wave mechanically from a high window
    set in the road's crook,

deep in a sloping mansard, recessed
    as into my forehead

hypnotized by its back-reflection,
    one in the eye, roguishly

for dust cut-&-panic. O fine redcoat
    in full costume

attend these beautiful stands, draw
    your rubric over the hills,

fading, starting to lick with fire,
    dabbed as if sable

hinting out beyond the ranged sights,
    spoils the plein-air, high-

lights Maroons on detail, backs bent;
at once the faders pull

down the voice of a love which lasts,
tuned to render unto Caesar,

defensive sickles ply, but a mahogany
panoptic sets off kilter

these hills for crucifixion, hills
that slicked with pleurisy

& lambent under their efforts, boil
the eucharistic cup juicy.

Where's the menial scrubs
a powderhorn, a lead bruise, where

the elderly wet-nurse
attending redshanks who now pule so

upon the foreshore? Ragged-robin
chokes their oaken ribs,

splattering the lower slopes, sked-
addling under split-level

sunsets, thin blood & tattered flags;
    the raspberry & redcurrant

hills retire behind a glassine leaf,
    manumitted to what hospital

or palace of arts for misty backdrop?
    Dredge canals, perform

    benedictions on our people;
clean your act up which ensanguined

    purrs stroked & fastidious
beneath the strokes of an agent eye

    brought forward in chains.
'I have created, making it serve,'

a sergeant says, 'Fit as a flea, was
    bankrolled, was swivelled

wildly, yes the chances were always
    there for a faithless kind,

the heart with lye from a burnt boat
    speeds the blood. Here is a

capstan your eye surmounts & kisses,
the smear on a timbrel

wealths have misbecome; it will wink
complicitly behind my back

as an index of lewd penitence, roll
one for the boys, admire

How impressive! father in his redcoat
ruddies reaches distant

skirl down to Montego Bay, Savannah,
Thomas Hardy country –

menacing the dusty childish passer
into redoubled hurrahs.

I knew it, I knew it, but ever after
plucked my walleye out

from its high casement, corner of it,
when it would miss its aim,

daubing itself with speciousness
& fully gorged on bloodshot

EXACTED

The ubiquitous now come home to roost
Who'd went without space to occupy,

but eat the loving hearts & the tinned
wallpaper, pressing on the lonely beds.

The endless road, that voluptuary,
tacked them to a portion of ill making,

terribly sweet it filled a front room,
such venom leaving never a trace

traced the children who were fitted up
to suit its dispersed purposes.

Here is the exact spot. I rest my case
& yours, & your mother's also

mouths out of its permanent abeyance,
saying, take what you wish to make

jam, of its contents, of its kind.
I rest my case. The trinkets & memento

spill in like soft rain in a soft chair
waving their flag for England;

that was the road & this the annexe,
niche for the soaked wayfarers,

so assiduously their way was re-routed.
Flesh & blood bears flesh & blood

only so far; in passing you & I bear
resemblance burnt as track-marks,

lifted & shed on the slack hemisphere.
Witness it, winged seedlings, for

example you might flutter & rest;
settle for these ransacked; we occupy

their holidays & strike root, we
stoop to eat within the vacated cabins.

COLOUR SWATCH

Elder sap
shrugged off its shoulder
bears in being let
                drop
                    phial,
a myriad single blossom head.
Terse
    as an unsocial guest
rakes over sand
were short with each other
                    unneap
myriad single rill.
                    No dry
amplification stilt
from day to tulip day
    stabilise interlace mode:
To define To except
  To transmit faithful bends
none by none,
slewed over wave-heads
            thick.
I, I heinous
            plot my slope
& rise & scream & snatch one.
Whatever has been so lopped,

water spent sensibly
by drip
pool,
wavelength, solves
once & for all time.
Statute:
Bits of this muck
makes where from stick.

Let any love its raggedness.

❦

And so the keys
shut down for the night
fingers
scarfed
into the ritual malediction.
Little Hydra combed
runs into a schoolyard
trigger-happy:
Who was it
spoke the shore
before nuptial waves
should rock themself?

Enter the last word
Enter broken impassioned
    mastersound
carrying metal scum,
weeds comb through each other,
  jostle for prime spots,
crowd the speech
shingle in soft triumph.

Ignorant
    the word cries
from out of their eutrophic
sex violence,
    muzzled into the LAN
network, catching at the
slave terminal fingers
clocking on,
            disjunctively.
There will never be a break.
    You will never find
that shore you smacked.

❦

So stay satisfied
   beneath the termite heap's
abecediary:
 the cell is completed,
the chewed paper
hardened about its tenant.
There's no place like home
   pullulates,
        Gently
disentangling rigid fingers
pokes a proboscis out.

❦

Says he, says you,
   undeterred, unphased.
     Straffed by a black
obmixture, pools
wink tarry on the palette,
grazed for seed by low-slung
   They like that,
just as it is.
By the ringway, legs will swing
   to the shore's slow
differences were ironed out.
They hit it off at once

    gloriously vanish.
Not before he says, says you
It must be oil
    Oil is all
  it might potentially be.

❦

Mother-ship
left empty, neuters earth,
  then parodies a dildo
Stage One thrust,
    unseats the chip.
  Fat volumes zero
& the certificates converge,

an interior sticks
half-way
  from hydrozoan fringe.
We lick its slimy new drug.
The spar that is clung to
transfixes,
      floats
like a beam in the eye lingers,

dragged for a heterotopia
    beaches right on cue.
   Voices
fluent at points of major stress
    fray the coaxial
stripped or tongue-tied
birds-eye graft,

regenerate out of their
mock armada
  over that waddling
              tumid sea,
flops down abrupt
& immerses
  Each us in our mort identity.

❦

There shall be no discrepancy,
each shall suit in
     common time, produce
promising empty space.

Apportioning fat zero,
     shot-up, they flee

those salt pans
condense in cobalt, tearing

apart terrible wrack
Lapelled for sign
of sanctity still gluey,
fraternise with a blink

riposte sneering 'Gone Away'
Then dissolve. A spin
treasure fills,
having rifled

through its stump for seed.
Anteing up towards life.
Dumps its empty tin
amongst already

heaving & inspected marsh.
One disgusting brew.
Substance
which will choke the ineffable.

❦

Milled
  to a control setting *(yes, that
satisfying clunk)*,
    hulled
with treated woods,
  a shipmaster's ten lashes
lick forms'
    occupants whose unison
pulls tides

        Tightening
the shoreline,
sweeping spongy roots
up above high-water mark –
  They are property
& squeezed for pharmaceuticals –
 Shaping
    from the white water,
runways
  Welting with green lights
the tropical pad:
      o my Maximus,
oftentimes a slave-trader:

  Deep-ocean fronds
float away
dreamily towards their trench,
      stretch & coif.

A smeary cellular mess
sea-lions browse & cuttles
Bladderwrack blisters
   languorously pop.

Trailed away
   or lumped on a horizon
what relies
on their genetic stock-in-trade
           treated
& shackled to their forms?
It concentrates vaguely,
   whatever it is
dreaming Amerigo off-course.

❦

Reverting home
   Nowhere
Abolishers of substance,
letting loose time re-find
   the post-obit place.

Turning out uncluttered
contretemps on main,
   passed often

slept away
to find blow in like
    hard vivid fog.

A way of knowing
    counter-traps in turn,
drew a school
    a sports-hall
congregates the outside
  team precursor,

  who still squats
the ghost of iron grilles:
others walk
    adversely
like rippling stained glass.

❧

  'I wish
there was a lizard
in my brain,' oil flag-wavers
  peel the limpid
patches
break along lines pre-scored,
    don't wish to overlay

their arc-en-cièle
    upon a fibrous loaf
consolidates the tainted grain.
    They grudgingly concede
that much-maligned
                cabbage-stalk,
urge a plate of dog,
mash with the back of a fork
their plantain

'I wish
there was a beauty
patch
    slewed piratically
across my snap-to-grid eyeball,
compelled'
            – like a red rag
    of neon
smarts through the inspection
    window the murk protects
Can't blot it out, won't descend,

Hue Luminance & Saturation
coded
    foodstuff shook upon the bone,
dive voraciously or
    decent, merely us,
spongify & as plankton glimmer.

Leader writers
shrug then pack their bags –
Let their ergot-burnt thesaurus

blazing up the penumbra
    muscle in to a focal point
& falsify:
'I wish
there was a basilisk
        inside,
invisible till spot-on
    cross-hairs
align to the deathful register.'

♥

There shall be a national grid
    faience turbine,
That scuttle
    Fire pouring forth
blank irises
    toil to charge its grid.

Contract
        Contribution
Irrespective

the mighty drops will drop
    measured, equatorial
force upon these groundlings
    stooping to clean out
a white mirror
      smudged
within its vanishing point.
This has to be the plasma
    force starts from,
    force returns to.

Rinsed in a glass craquelure
     wrack sticks
dries & snaps
where the irises once grew.
    A blank pool
ought to be preserved
          asphalt, ought
to detain the heel,
snag the apt eye
    whose present allure

imperiously plumes the sand,
closes in boxes, grids,
  picturing
dark-eyed
vicissitude to cap them all
    will be their motivator.

Every humble soul
      sinks
into its eyes' joint,
manufactured
deep in its Whites Only mirror.

SOLFATARA

It is June & the bluebottles start to blunder
about a phantom space who carries in front of you –

darting out with his/her cynical smile, no hangups
loom their deniers, straight now, lesbian now,

deodorised the spiritual flesh is spooned away
in a rattle of old cans where wasps drink & drown

black inside, white inside, male, female, banded,
bloody brilliant, stupid, swiss rolls, roulades.

Loose covers & the upholstery split. Hill-farmers,
browned-off as the magnolia, stacked & bruised

pillows for hand-me-down, tied to their format's
custom & practice, slippery with their fast spoil,

parley the hooped timber back into wholesomeness
fresh as a brake of conifers, timeless values

breathe new air, setting to rights the community!
scry over a ladle of porridge, authentic food,

the gorsed of druids, a morris, the orthodox choir
calendric like a square-dance dip & bow & stay

in fixed continuity, in servile cloth, o spirit!
Where a break is, where dense destructive focus

pinned inside the blouses of magnolia girls
foreheaded in broidery, well spoken wouldn't speak

except for catch-as-catch-can intermittent wisps,
cracks out a folded square, its *point de capiton*

a star severe as raspberries on the flat of a loaf!
dangles now like a tampon from such clean limbs

plump their flowery pillows filled with potpourri,
o blithe spirit, whomsoever your baton stabs

unable to stir the on-the-spot, this rooted June,
droves of bright green minibuses shall trundle

breezily to assist the followers, famine-weak,
husks & sticks & eyes which brittle with a desire

for The Truth, snap-to to tow an implicit line.
In concentration camps they'll get fed languages,

a Latvian injection, plain English, a controlled
trial of Welsh, cawl to satisfy. The fatedly

kaleidoscopic chew it, now Croatian, now Chinese,
hyphenated, compromised, anorectic, gathered

pleats whereby the forcefield brought to bloom
at a clock-stroke, strews the foamy road & decks

with their vicissitudes a dying motley. Dismantle
their hearts off their sleeves, folk embroidery

they got stuffed with, their freely-floating
scent gutters & fills the wicker they preoccupy.

THE ADAM SMITH INSTITUTE

Their automobile crackles like the human rind
creaks defectively, laps diminutive, flows brittle.

Black flambeaux feed on plastic leather both
look the trimmings & upon the medium treacherous.

Mass appropriated, sears the wire-heated screen
were red satin drapes opaque as wax, fancy the hot

evidence pored over by a stiff-ply sheet, Europe,
hyping up their fever, firing handguns for a DJ.

The sirens & a neighbour bell shall call-&-respond;
this is their shithouse, nothing remains itself,

the children have been parcelled as though doves
waffle in the throats of other, laughing children.

Free of outside pressures, from the autocade
thick with the smell of spilt sperm & local honey,

when June catches up with them they'll chuck paper
balls like fortune cookies, the journalists

throwing their jeeps eagerly at void chicanes,
flatten a crumpled rebus against the seat & giggle.

Nostrils begin to prick, to smithereen caustically.
Summer notes. Some fearfully afflicted stare

sightless at patches recombine behind their whites,
that prisoned fortune beast struggles down a loop

held like a pine cone, tight within their thighs'
predictor World Bank skinflints snuffle at & poke,

spark & smell of stone fire built the new exchange,
blasphemously stir, entice through a back passage

god in thinly scattered oaten mix, a shattered
gold church, Aurora fallout for my brainbox floats.

I've been the journalist of this pause to regroup,
personally: Some things you just can't naturalise,

sometimes you can't be coy, platitudinous or vatic;
autopsies will unpick, disgustingly delicate,

a few leaves, grasses burnt in a distended stomach,
ripped apart hopefully to get at the free toy car.

SLIP GENERATIVES

You fill the gap, you cross the barrier, bridge the divide;
& what became of the fond rift, did it too smooth away
like milk bellies, spoiling all with comprehension, rapt &
briefed beforehand with the stone of its slotted parents?
Top-down, bottom-up, no firmament confounds nor does a deep.

Steam haunts its lowest ebb & cloud clusters at the highest;
how an explosion scatters light before it, wipes a slate
shimmering where lamps design the crossing places, grit
counts you in a sling that feathers above the waterfall.
Seldom you will pause as you stretch out its fleshly spool

launches into limitlessness. Here is brick, double-baked.
Here is amber, here is pitch to smear your arms, salve lips,
tallow to stuff resounding ears. You stand like a flypaper.
You hold a trowel & with it you daub every lost saying.
Sun blinks, a river below skips, solitary you'll slap the rink.

THE TRUTH TABLE

Divorce the trapdoor from that precipice it gave onto;
too many couldn't Infants who chug round a building-site,
wisps of steam infused above an earth an ill-detected
threesome shifts & wrinkles, blinker a promiscuous eye,
the faceless semidetached, The Thing Is, set in concrete.

Once scuttled underneath its surface quick & occlusive,
within the tapetum opaque, of many ways to skin a rabbit
experience showed this too plainly, catseyes dazzle like
an asphalt inland sea, as most rill like water on a steep
industrial road, once the lightning plays to no effect.

Rinse it interfluently then, neither stint when reproach
glistens off tough jelly, the moral & marrow blink too
in reconnoitring, like a lightship all astray bounces off
not conscience, loose little shreds of fear, crazy dots
admonishing to highlight their stiff cloak of watery ruin.

He is the non-lover, surfaced in these vagaries comport
over a face facing he who faces truth with a truthful mien.
A spring seeps, but not from the eye which is varnished
with the day's embrace, it sings in its buried channel
always before his seat they approach tearfully & lidless.

BELSTONE

Carelessness will cost them lives, already does with millipede
precision. A fire engine screams, close to the breakage suite.
Patched up, pieced together, we articulate on foray, searching
for that velvet actuarial bag. We're whistling with our lumps
across the mainstay paludal state of grace, stumbling to heal.

A helicopter's blades struggle against the molasses darkness.
A starfish frolics over repeated sand, tracing its faint nebula.
Nothing is fanciful, nothing can be dismissed now out of hand.
The receivers are ill with their own literalism, & a malarial
fever stirs the agents of a prudent reckoning to jump the heart

infidelically. By rote against the stream, look to their profit.
Stone by stone the cairn of the past which hardly weighed, is
made off with by heartsearch. They live at the angle of fracture.
Their ghosts lay stepping-stones on the swamp & walk chilblained
with the hot little numbers, stones applied from a seething pot.

ATTENTION AND INTERPRETATION

A treatise divides between its several heads, yellow
safe as its green is matter-of-fact, ladies-mantle
bunched lustrous jar, converges & is close to oceanic –
No more no more. The earth bread, the millet, maize,

the repeated cattle voluble as though on cranes' legs,
where shall these be put? A telephone put its reply
summarily before a priest calling, stands & clicks
divining-bones like callipers, adjusted so as to nod

agreement but in a separate context. It is a protocol
followed by true, farsighted men. Their fine yellow
hegemony spreads, in pollen unconstrained but keeping
bounds, lilts towards the future thought to include

a number of specifics. Take the colourful antidote
to irony, the sexual check on starvation, shuttles of
feverish remedies would swerve through roseate water
plump the little object I which wallowed & withered

& wallowed again on the lam like an ECHO virus; take
that ragamuffin seeds & multiplies, cursed to remain
orphaned ever within its own likenesses – it is clear,
is it not, is it not, is it not, blue heaven sweats.

UNBIDDEN

Favourite wings have put his name to this Favourite wings
his pious devasting, no right to silence which is calculated
finely to degrees of insolence or guilt says that person
You never loved me, all I was was hinged as a microphone.

Devout as the ace of spades I too never flourish corruptly
too tried to fray the strands of complacent multicore
boost anonymity as their calling card like sleek legs cross
How could you do this to me, where is the simple repeat now.

Fuzz starts to run inside the instrument that no polish
needed never a blurt no never a coarse sound from his reed
but ache mellifluously as a stream of yearning ducats
Trust you to carry it off, the soft soot lined the fireplace.

Meat smiles & rests its O I would scuttle the syllabary on.
The stamens loll, the bells nod, the first wax flowers
hold their peace for the season which is predicted to the day.
Don't ever come back, this note is repeated in the woods.

TABLE MANNERS

What underlies is what also has to billow forth
disconsolately true, & while trailing on surfaces
will never tear, shrivel, ball, only will return
Clingfilm had been the bones' wrapping floats.

So what she dispenses also were the simple facts
of love which is incontrovertible but unproved
It coats the heaving, the inner articulations,
returning to gently wrap her face in brilliance.

But I feel the fine sufferance rip away from bone
stricturing my body with a long soft sigh, do
this undifferentiated, never leave my mouth or
break surface, this would be too hard a gloss.

from **SARN HELEN**

/

bayoneted. If any will hear the truth must cling best
avoid blow dragonflies, cling on by nail-feasance
over a cataract which scours a giant curtain wall,
or was it short-of-time shrunk the unseeming aimless
river to a bank's sediment? Common seals luxuriate
transmitters pinned behind their perked-up ears,
breezes buffet from all directions Body-build them
into a race of top achievers, filing across hillsides
mewl within their gathering blades, a scopophilia
shrink-wraps the forest in its retailer's proud image
Preserving it while it speeds, dragnetting seagulls,
seagulls, choughs, a tinkers' brood they desolate
with far cries. Filaments shall creep though bated
shear the nucleus, threads by which I still revolve
shook where a deadeye holds the swarm by scent,
from bracken rising augural, on white stuff lightsome.
Bindings dishevelled dry & tighten on their windlass
mummify, screwing a bridge's tension dip & straight,
machines tramping open cropped ground beneath
go incognito in a high-wire infant parsing T-cells
Nose squashed on a greyprint, how will molten tar
fuse the cracks the drought shall visit? Canefrogs
jump the continent, leaf through springy signatures

closer than a razor-blade's width. Co-dependency
was our sick tract, gluey exudate we thought to pill,
thought in lieu of reagent so a pancake could solidify
honeycombed poor silicate, quivering to adjust
hand-to-hand remedial lets the day-out skaters pass
They throng the pentangle straw-fringed, slip-slide
through turnstiles like windows read seasons' entry.

Stronger the differences yet more shall they even out,
locally stabilised against their brushed & rolled-on
variety of roots affiliations. Affording scope for
trapped bubbles closing above the issue decompress
on the running crack we learnt to compère, calling
after names we programme to overfly. Love of Mike
streams from a capsule still might generate Mike
Who. Repack his space with sex toys & a calculator.
Being obdurate ground a chain of buckets empties.
A scraping machine drew its blade on protuberances.
The vacuum sipped slowly like the seamed vessel
girds itself & counts on Count on a decent return,
farting, a Wizard of Oz gale restocks what billows
caulked but incapable of self-evidence. As it imbibes
of the downdraft, belching short, distressed bouts,
send-storm shall abate & the crows-nest jiggle high-
vaunts to see behind lifts the nose of a coming storm,
compassed too by the arena. Drop its grey bundle
like on a scaffold television sours & is less buoyant.
But it seems their ionized stuff might over-rehearse

its early state of mobility, a platoon of engineering
squaddies drilled in straight lines for a lemming wave
spot & fox & it is their Passchendaele implodes in
reinforced trenches. The plasma sheath like a condom,
they start to expel communicative a flock of gulls
outperforms his spec, he will be a founding premise
this week of what he shortsees. Rewind the meter
dangles its supplement inside a white & careful box.
We took the ladle to the punchbowl frosted in a clear
tame stream. Around my arm the air was strapped.

❦

/

Trot, extortionate file in line with the hills' flutework,
at the start catenary but their rising, thickened stave
snags in seedheads & finches & wool. Take all to sum,
so to wind up penned by the smoke of its far issue
Dumbhead formation does it envy such stir as crows
seem to make, tussling the body-bags to steep the air,
worry & pick at husks from summer's grindstones
litter the path, amidst rows of tuned pegs is humming?
Immigration officers sit in a shed roofed with flies.
The land is heavy but the yams flinch when male light
wrenching connectibles, wrinkling like their lugs
bucked against a parapet were floored. Way to go,
but thought's topography subtends the erotics of risk
tumbling down bright shiny parcels, sexually launch
metalled squadrons so far out & multiplying, half-
cow propagates their halo peels off to prick its score
Notice the fancy stitches concentration overshoots.
That to which the burning grasses yearn for order
nosedives. Vital chaining must confirm rank potential
Whoever snatched up with a hook you can't complete
its overview the calves cross-strap in aerial tropes
quilt like the backing clouds, fending off a close fit
Deliverance will unstitch as though to stretch a point:
the enzymes that look lively with their Fastforward
Recue, swap between the piles & name each mess
At the crossroads is a kind of awning gobbles stupidly,

totally aware, varietal blank. He farts & belches,
sequentially he cracks his face but does not spread
Many lines were free, stripped them out like veins
choke the hull of the isthmus. Flex & go. Protrusive

crazed as he would through crack propagation radiate
the knowing one over & over, hop-skipping a key
round luggage-feeders, cheesewires the oyster hinge,
coiling into their breastwork fouls up the collect
outlandish scatter charts, labile to mislead, depose,
fluttering stilt lash tints for an iridescent semaphore.
On the left flank dismounts a flatter squarer thicket.
Skaters cut dendritic drainage patterns, who beset
in bridgework a folding half-way. Whatever approach
of coarse grass vaccinates his gums, what approach
panics the thready cistern might joke-gush but saw
far-offs off to their prospecting – one cluster went
straight for implementation Why not, its halo-effect
flees Ionic pillars to illumine pegs unstrung. Inter-
mitent claudication bends knees to the bottom line
cracks in a drought of catechism once darkness hits.
Trench-foot privates had back-firing from their slope
sensor array retards with pleading upheld hands
warted in ripe pods. Snap snap snap unattributably
philander for the truth of it I'd switch path to path
down the fused projection nets have shaken out
its spectres of flesh & blood, dose by dose released
re-bodied force their opening through its time-head

Or ever they stabilize as if a short-rotation coppice
ripped between currents, proud & foaming. Flimsy
as I am I burrow the fallopian waste of my making.
Throat like sandpaper grates on a brusque valediction
flags in so doing gathers pace. Granted its width,
its breadth & distance, what calibration serves to fold
edgeless, radiant, erasive, their saved up fervencies

from *SACCADES*

Sunlight seeps component hours therefore forbear to set.
    One only accompanist, it twanged
the white fingers will embraid then shake their tally open
    like tap sticks; & the fob of the guardians
kicks in to chatter, balance wheel spin, escapement clutch,
    but are not what they angled for,
attraction/repulsion reaped the light these would uphold.

Gaps narrow, fingers sweep their sensory weft according
    to what shade jumps hyperactive,
like a loom clanks silently they oil the nodding kiss grove.
    Waive the near approach of
silk slip, hessian scour, velvet might hold back but slopes
    damaged for the thought of it.
Behind, a lozenge licks out the sun. Light no more seeps

its automatic crop. By shortfall only though it cottons on
    egg-ridden like a moist pad
chewed following precedent, in double twist wound tight:
    what could be more hurtful
than this event foreshortened? Mechanisms start to whirr,
    the heliograph to jerk & sputter,
lengthening at verticals but flits down treads & banisters.

Flat against the rhythm track the unified theory advances,
      each sentence starts 'and', & spurious
connectives reconcile: all are migrant, the whole resource
      scarred by this pathology. Place
each face down, will memorize each long enough to copy,
      slipping between rollers, through
horizontal gates to slide into Tray B unruffled, creaseless:

hissing copies scrawl walls in tick plumets of feuillemorte.
      Favour them, their outgo squares
flesh with stone, the chiselled profile lining up its shadow
      claps-to like a door hangs light,
& fruit trees will rotate rotting cherries & bletted updates –
      plush below their shared-office
accumulation, ghosts on the walkway tiptoe their canopy.

So what is this catches in the throat? Like a cistern rattles
      rightly, complete, fit-for-purpose –
like a physical remnant tugs or overblown insipid melody
      circulates the wilful stalk:
stops in its tracks, blushes white, it can't keep up; thumb-
      marks complicate such sound,
glittering like quartz will restructure the operating system.

Out of a pit below their ramp, scraped metal may release;
      up in the shelving arrays

pneumatic grunts discharge, a thought regulator kicks in;
        on the back of a trailer bike
a CV in its pizza box; skies imperial whisk & chronology
           spirals through the air, a reading
across domains ties down functions wish to blow, period,

drives exchange by one for one occludes the rip blow-out.
        This device chokes any interference
received: the hand snakes its needle & thread or spanner
        stubs against invisible little jets –
that windy scamp would transfix the marshalled muscles
           along their file-paths,
wish-merriment throbs error messages, pulsing in hippus.

The universals race, pushing aside presets, the full heart
      launched off involuntarily,
hold filled with fine skins, cowries, gems which were eyes.
      Raise the new capital & chorus.
Its dizzy shown frontage marble-clad, is a Potemkin wild
          with ghosts, admits nobody:
no report is current but that which shivers the tin islands.

Where disks had jiggered out for counters I spread news
      through the vacant boardroom,
breathing on mirror surfaces. A scheme is by such token
      not a person (or vice versa).
A stone is not a stone but a hot hearth capping emptiness
      had squandered their titanium
rib-stuffed vertebrae. Curtains behind them jacket lustre,

in key bunches bear results, indexes & standing in public,
      the compensatory voices hang
are shed in four-decker tape is spirals onto the shiny rug.
      They burn there, their secretary
wipes the tape between her ears & fingers Shall this fizzy
          die-for-it discriminate
in the medium term, dredge one message for its director?

Non-stock voices shake aspirin boughs, resentful overlap
      & flapping coats will see bulk.

How faulty was their take-up (both ways) would cover it;
   a full course of stone is laid
against absconsion held to cost. Full-pelt a bracelet flexes
         the nervous cord, so help you
part implies; stones rattle surrogate, Assisted Conception.

'Open' is their gauge who would master the presentation
   skates dazzling surfaces.
A marble headboard blinks over a bed of algedonic gravel.
   Fire-ants raise like scabies
rights of the so-signed in their runes, a long flame yearns
         to skitter from its funerary,
a will-o-the-wisp dancing over the marshes behind sings.

Click or snap or so the rifle seeding on all fronts its hydra
      mayhem over drear, spitting smoke
from its puckered bay, fomenting what it had needs must,
      the sun streams still, particles
will irritate a voided chamber: But sun can never compile
      its expression & will fizzle out.
White fingers carry this less glimmer & snap sorrily fault.

The indulged fault by its lower quay could uplift distress.
      A high fault locates & kissing dark
resigned the self-slipped skull to treat its difference, sum:
      skin of a rapt servility
swelled so taut anticipates one round can pierce, burn or
      burst soul recoil on through,
derogates to watch, trembling admires a mensual routine,

bolts out universally to circle & pin down with fiery seed.
      The sun suggests there are worked,
gone terrifying reasons underlay such incandescent trace
      outlives the mouth. One single shot
or sheaf had set its more conniving course, one small dab
      post-hoc would shrink
to a mascle sported like a pendant in the eye, a set comma

blinks brushed with webs to contain the reaction, caustic
      threads of spit were a cream's horn.

Here a spice engobbed disports a breath sheathed within
        & invites one sidelong foil.
Nutmeg bloats the mace, slicks into the rasp o imperious
        mentor kneaded out of shreds
beats within its col of salt, a reef below this burning floor

throws rubbery stalks like a devil lobs their tracer-shells,
        finding work for the hard saps
wrung & rubbed & budded whenever a tear might swell
        offshoots out from it, ruining
its particulate world was its band never brought to proof,
        never was previously disturbed.
Save where the kiss is thickening fiery on a cocked finger.

Obstructed in the inner costume of its violences this rock
      was pudding stone, the genius
an upsurge of analgesics will beat against but not resolve;
      so pavement light must swerve –
but bring no cheer to those who hate its vaunting & lope
             next to it like a loose wolf,
blow on blow entreat as in wounds they could remember.

Investigate the ivy ripped from walls, whose bristly scabs
      will crown the pan-pipe shit-
stirrer, hands-off down had shoved his metered followers
      onto a scruffy dog-shit patch,
kicking about a stone where their details are held in store.
           Downwardly causative,
wedged between a rock & no place is the so-abject pillow.

Spirals in the concrete which they called Sarajevo flowers
      sheet-bombarded, corrugate the
gabbles of a hectic lip that fridge-vacant still must satisfy
      its thick & repugnant moss.
Water! Water! Fetch me my chips! Let the infirmities fill
         my dreamt hollow: they shall en-
crust over an electronic billboard as dreamt in contraflow.

What is their crackling purse so empty with? Candelabra
      rookeries raise up their cups

triple-decked in squabble, spurts of gravel see them soar
        in their communities, ancient dialling
redress settles two nights forward flat like a palette-knife
        slides into some bedroom
as a squint square blackening on the spread, for this was

their matter for choice, intense to overtrick such sombre
        premonition yolked. Endorphins
rush to neutralize the bright-rimmed cloud, frail warmth
        a tense earth strains against,
left to work out shoots had eked light had begged a crust
        from lipped bowls of effluent,
cradled by the disconnected & superb darkness mossing.

Try a black baize door closes yawns 'open' in its defence.
        Moss dries to a mangy crust,
a lunging chisel clatters before the draught-swung gates
        Then will you see this visitor
towards the hearth, no, go upstairs, to the lump of stone
        won't you? Arterial blood
soaks his blonde pelt, it is a stab in the dark, a phosphene.

❦

Spraying & feathering toner, rainbowing into shutdown:
    as if the carbon watch-cloak
manoeuvres slant to draught, pursues an object will shift
    glamour to what it fancies, –
but coin of the realm from a tinny horn still can propose
    chucking more, the windpipe
lifts its song from the dark, back where it yearns to shut.

The least vapour became droplets. Placate in sap velocity
    off the block lips cuneiform.
Amongst collapsed stars amino acids coil matter venting.
    The hellhole, the tough shit,
chill or scorching as the crosscurrents flayed their shred
    colourful spectra, ground noise
for which there had been no foreglance but a metre taped

lifts compatibly, from her bag is someone incriminating
    swirling out in bias cut –
chewing a bumflap, inturning in darts, the hobbledehoy
    of dip, of breath thermals rise
in red lines & gilts cross-revetting their punched leather
    stiffens under notice.
Armoured contour in line, peering past a modular set-to,

that's how she lost her rags & found them, wafting stack
    castoffs like as next of kin
harvest & barter lucid pain to restore pain to steep dark.
    The collapsed brightness

broods like an eye sucks out the socket, smirched clouds'
               shadows confiscate a wink
or some derogatory spark, its skintight accent fluttered

no more than is deliberate, cap. Wriggle its scud piping
            deep where the unsingable
cannot be swallowed or hoisted to straddle attendant air,
            catches nothing but self-consumes
in panting, bronchial flames billow were sent randomly,
               continually sounding off
unimpeded that might breath & velleity block or impart.

FROM A TERRACE IN TUSCANY

Clearly but this cartouche,
was it an exhaustive bitter train
      flares from the seed –
even such geometry as
shakes its ventured flower out?

Why not prefer that orb whose
unreflective case
    empties
hot rubbish in the remembrance,
a long time
    past to this canonist
hybridizing bleached songs.

Section one, section forever,
    & the interminate
length of sentence was the germ
    in repair, unrolls,
rubs within the capsule
protecting it.

Diligent or contrary? Re-
pollinate strip or thirsty spike
      engineer
snap chemical clock

also known as
    have the best bits for mine.

But you must buy a key next year,
    they last one season.
Light must be shed
through the definitive leaves,
    & a particular case
stabilize their flickering

makeup like the positional
winged ants
mote by mote plume as completely.
    Is it nothing
rasps, raps, the chisel-
plumpnesses bursting to stick,

all slow dredge enzyme?
    Their chewing-gum
parades, the starch, the sperm
    rip iridescence
down to the tasked traffic, edging-

blade honeycomb run by the mill,
will thicken sky, dispose of
    flights of cellophane.
Their filthy light
sings through any such delivery:

scar taste was the only distance
unrolls

    Cut the brilliant flower.
Fade.

LONDON FIELDS FROM AFAR

Whether market forces
or upsurge in confidence
          picks up their heels,
the drop-shadow slope makes
a grounded look
before the tilting windows.
              Why then scurry
over the fens like crazy hearts
    dressed in sun-
          shine or moon-allowance.

          Windows open so far.
Misery belts out the sunken vowel
stupid in its pot of
          Now Jump
as legislation or style altogether
state their own state.
          Jump & land in shadow
breaks their legs
then flounder like clouds stop
over the Amazon.

Watch out for skin texture.
At ground level light goes turbid
on the young thick wheat.

Where did the allergen
spray rise,
        over no advance?
This is to burn, a spy glass
kindles & will blister
        to admire or even pluck.

But stay.
        Affluence in a capsule
will trump the next hand.
                Moonshine has less
    going for its fisty shafts,
its spill
        of antic vowels
than the canter of such chains
the sun against the skin is locked into –

phase transition. Dust rises
beside the mauve ledge & marble
        hits liquidity. Striate
over the mineral hills
plumes of vapour
blot down, their lustre
swiped between the legs' withdrawal

or as glamour counts,
but fruits weight & the granaries
shut your gob or gape

resequenced to be sterile
shall not, can never detain.
Run with the refugees
along Mare Street
to London Fields, Elysium:
Ensoulment is an instant's work
The ears pop
The eyes water.

SOME MARKING &
YELLOW HIGHLIGHTING

I carried a forkload which was warm
& not heavy –
wispy as candyfloss.
    & said This is the very best
I can lay my hands on.
If a gold dab were to hand
I could
    go in now, let this slide off
& be on fire without ignition.
I could take you at your unsaid word.

But I had to use that particular word.
At once the pitchfork
    grabs a pill went down
the wrong way. Whichever.
    About sixteen years
she can expect in the circumstances.
Keep your bit of kindle
    to yourself, maybe chew
for a retaining mess
    Like horsehair
bonding plaster. Up to you, to drivel,

weep maybe or squeeze a blob of
cadmium. The high sky
sends to shelter, weather will change,
clouds reconfigure
black, red & gold over Davos,
    blown by an ill wind
sharper figuratively than any wind.
  Substance
may function as a transmitter of pain,
    dream
flush the overstock. Whichever.

I'll take food when it crosses your lips,
  not the rack
lain across the horizon,
     a great deal absolutely
gags where a forkful reunites.
    This is the only
place left for us, a relative freedom
in its encircling walls,
crackles like straw behind that chicken
wire left over. How golden it is.
    How freely it burns.

RESTRINGING

The strings have to be pulled tight,
to the hilt the agile moves
    Like a cello
    a squash racket/
break-beams for the intruder,
security gates unfolding outward
knew who this beguiles
    by temperament.
Girls laughing along quays
below hills drawn spontaneously
    to echo them,
are penned in together.

Happiness tugged at loose knots.
If summarily I trailed,
    thought-through almost
before knowing my own thoughts
    Almost tripped
    Almost guided
into the echoing undervaults,
still gentian
still the green shot strung on vines
insisted on a responsiveness.

Coal sets the limits against clover.
Sculpture however clumsy.
The jackal & the wolf
forsake their god-speed, float
above my head as though swatting
giant ears,
& the boom out of quarries
searching for antiphony.
Give it time. Give it
        necessary distance.
        Case star core
languidly sings between girls,
permeant if not original,
halting, but continue
passing over the loved face,
the highly strung which tangled,
husked or shaped bits
feel, tasting
        each's near-capitulation –
scraps of song known well,
these were known in circles
becoming mazy disputatious roots.

Off the terrace the diapente rings
Off the terrace a blue note
curves the flight
magnetically to its interval
        So too resin

coltran or cobalt
draws behind a chador on
the flat-out, on the main drag/
   erratic & purposive,
hotspotting the limbic waste, burns
what will be memory
through coarse stuff,

by rote becomes by heart,
  the catch, the glint
against the contrast medium: Who
this might be I croon to myself.

from **CASE IN POINT**

§

Little question point will revisit, countersunk
mark I accept I palm, tongue-kiss
migrant but ensconced point, which

way you cut, proportionately, cross-
rolls its specification
keeping something back: Fly not their button

prompts to act like mistletoe,
not the membrane dot provides access,
neither remembrance would, its aphid crowd

sticking thirsted to the point
occludes any pore or the skin water-repellent:
the question ripcords from its POV

but is the same spangled entreaty
placoid to light,
the same deflector so much its own, re-frames

roots. Hide their tracks, shred paper, captions
devastate the pile:
is myriad singleton

behind the face, not as if sewn
up or styptic where its lopped branch, its knot
of mistletoe is a back-formation yes?

§

Such screens pan out veins as day's eye closes;
like an unbroken clickclack
toils through the horizon ring, feeds

filature to its underside, diverted, bled across,
opalescent when focus pulls. Flowers
like taken by the off-centre

sidetracking necked or stitched like swarming
mandarin ducks, wear blatant
fanfares for their patches, polarised,

all resort levered in by the dull spot shone up
point to point, cross-threaded. Blank
bleeding hearts, primroses can-

not anticipate, roses make the fist
that will not blurt, pout
or gulp after a show of resistance – the daisies

scatter much hereabouts, bossing
out yellow sex centres were they to make bold
whites in pink blush, a signet

were anti-daisies, aliased, in
their own points reticulated. These they were.
These is. Rolled neatly.

§

A bag is what you sneak your hand in, gloved
with fat but a box would have been useless;
for example a foreman sidles up,

adipose by half. He strives for that consistent
yellow will coat the wall Phooey:
Better it was wrinkled & flaking,

was held in a bag, a bag that never resentful
fetches or festoons. Holds grain.
Holds money. Holds the shopping. Sooth

to handle, shopping grows a skinny hem
scrunched on one side transfixes. Dream stuff
hung from ragged lips will tempt

autumnal bags. Air itself seems never enough
insurance on its own, save if
plastic-coated, bidding fair to hold.

A bag belongs, the bag to carry its bag carries
the fat of the whole intent. What boxes
do, comparatively? Echo the point:

Fragile: what you want is best
avoided & in avoidance shines whole intent.
Your bag was sealed with a side hasp.

§

So like any civilian, point. Your box contains
grape samples or amphetamine, it holds
expiring breath & faded air,

colour will bring them out. Seriously that box
is a treeless forest, sighing
away its wood. Trees are but decorative

torsade, for the box a colour readout disloyally
has laid bare, so fill its clearing
with calm questioning in dark blue.

Across the bowl-curved analogue, vine tendrils
stretch a colourful chord
to twang & pollen flies inventively,

clogging wind apparatus, bestows its touch, a
fingertip erotics. The sharpest rind
the tongue anticipates, rind

about a space voluteless, scarcely can compete
with the blue of a box, the rind only,
previewing a display of displays.

Such blue tablets, such black box decodes, air
racked on affirmatives, these
the vine disrupts with lightest fingers.

§

A DJ puts that groove down in a private club.
A scratch held apart so as to incubate.
A vigilante takes his heat. Hotshot.

Feet compress the forest trail, its underthatch
        /horsehair sags aloof desirable
Where's the pocket. Ripped out.

That's to provoke not some resigned attitude
uniformly strikes
lash for eyelash, feedback in the cubicle

detects its always front makeready thin stock,
soaks in saliva,
soaks in acid, in urea
        Soft-shoe
        plantation

rowan splash, photoperiod burst,
        fingering a blunder mass installed
base in that booth sucks the silt back & forth

mending & re-mending what
lemon spare part So let flatten
                So a regular pulse
locks & re-dilates,
sweeps the sand now marked out for runway.

SIDESHOW

What shall divide me now?
Unpick the seam
                  the wound
whose guts went out,
      conquering space.
My wound has been crowded
full as a corpse of self

Beside me the hum continues
      breaking into song –
no, hardly amiss within
day's labour & the body's
      exactions –
        this is not cleaned up
or wrapped or binned,

but sustains its note
      alongside, & keeps time
for alibi that its droning suits.
         Tight neck
lets balloon or shrivels
marks or in qualities,
dominant all the same

as thinking carries forward
     down its forks
by Type & by Creator.
For they have both to be
plied, & the knife
     too as needs must;
& these were the pent cutlery
thought's song works with,
worrying a tip
     under the matted-
down stitch, easing
the categorical thread.
             Unhook
its prosodion I, no longer taut.

FUNK QUALMS

Stuffed like a scarecrow, are these
genuine boundaries I asked as between
tillers of earth, or signals I hope not.

If there is no bone it is a breast, if
no nipple it is an open pit I am clawing.
A decompressor was candied in blood.

Yes I want to have this so I can swap
for something ephemeral I can now miss
that badly it will be mine for always.

MERCATOR

A lovers' shadow, thumbed
from waxy & ambitious
skins advances to the knoll,
casts its bolt, sees eye to eye,

the sticking place is always
darling that reluctant
ever to seal over, coercive
pulls their troubled shade.

Merry co-star will deflect
as though impregnable,
spot spent position-taking
startles to the bigness there,

taps the shadowy mound
loosening caught heels.
Darling sweat the loud
thunder, let its rolls extend

crescendo on crescendo,
flattening a carefully-cut
circle. In San Diego, loaded
sequencers conceive cells.

CITÉ SPORTIF

Cité Sportif: testing aerobically, by step change
sponsors the crisis so the constant will bricks burn.
Unilateral gives a hand blade-first to a domestic
falange hampered by no fingers follows through/
losing feet halted
lost half her face.
Spare this without fail
curated utmost measures clowning cutoff guns,
torn-blossom aesthetics, paper-eaters
                              cannot obstruct
an armed proxy, artfully arrange their clippings.
- Oxygen of suppression
- Suck-out from the dug-in
- The tell-tale account switch
wrist-flashing lane IDs
neon-clocked down the strip totally what stamped
intelligence docket couldn't, can you stomach, you
have no stomach which must be superscription
documents sent ahead, to add up to a fateful boy
dubbed incorrigible had from birth or by neglect
        traded for time in blocks,
        the flat soles cushioned,
        the Uzi clips were shucked –

options bud to bud maturing, evidence this moon-
face freewheels a urethral crook, heads for home,
made up, really made, what respect resections him:
His birth-repeat spatters
the real stomach contents not some installed shit.

- Eat & cannibalise
- Pastry-cut trainer soles
- Eat stadium tropicália
- This mental block

fly-posted, tag-painted to dissolve, dressed to cal-
culate aggressive daub, organize MP3s:
would an intelligence captain tremble at their well-
heeled, feasted song opening with bloody boxes
trodden down, stamped out?

His own work. Solely. Stamps
authoritatively.
Native soil. Folds
plain enchiladas. Sunk ballads to regurgitate, for-
fend the fast food he'll have to chew then slew!
subversively, orbs crusted in portentous sugar,
seized scallops, interrogation suit has gold thread
detailing, monogram tweezered through each

face-grating swabs
these legs, these hands, a man will round the bend
for first place on the last lap,

mount the impregnable dais
A hard day
A Riefenstahl

fitness course
between holes could the bunker, could the green,
this hole draw back the skin like a parachute/
clingfilm-wrap what they spilt/ drove from earth
the fox & all proxies bearing parts in their mouths

I think not
I think not

CITÉ SPORTIF

Theatrical in their casting out, their eyes strew
engineer the woman they'd once conceived
adorns now bus shelters, nightclubs, wheel-
chairs with drawn-up hearts & carriage, hers
& others', match iconoclasts in rose-red cities,
holy place overlaid on holy place overlaid
where to go round the more scopes the whole.
        You are driving but across its range
        throwing up, throwing up.

Turn a corner down, turn down its dog-eared
corner, take the corner to see the velodrome
assemble all loose objects including humans –
in L'viv say, then copy, wire New Record Poll,
double crows-feet emblazoned on the sheets,
the critical targets trackside huddle, count,
tagged to every object twisting for aerial skier.

Alive, the broidered initial
but splints your bones' collision.

Using a proprietary measurement scheme,
what takes away wipes the grimace entirely,
nothing gives birth but count in time stitches
• Hold the torchlight
• Hold the explosion
• Replenish dugout stores.
Civic-minded recycling, how does that differ,
        bring the choke-points to collection
points he pokes at groggily,

once more round the block
        shell casings slip & crunch, delivery
systems keep integrity whatever use the spent
        are put towards. A ring-
dove perches in the florid
        Chinese, Persian or an English
orchard as here without number. Cherry
        mess, cherry tat, cherry blossom
stuck like cotton wool overlays year on year
low-level uranium.
                        Slung in sentimental waste
                        the flesh softens,
                        overwrites & overwrites,
                        pulses & contributes.

Zealous beside the Arno, Thames, North River,
tippling the Bekaa Valley's finest, scoffing up
stuffed pigeon, slid the layers, keyed in layers
overlay a deep-down Sepulchre, the Alhambra,
Holiday Inn where photographers holed up
receive messages from way uptown, young men
rounded up, having their measurements taken
    end up in the first position,
    high school kids up for it.

CITÉ SPORTIF

The flat mandorla pulses painfully beside the basin,
beside Manchester City,
    beside Yankees be-
side deer trainers, NFLP trainers, & at the rim,
about the cindered margin triumph heel to toe
        Cripps trainers,
UDF trainers, Death Row™ trainers,
kangaroo trainers, the personal trainer jabbing this
clipboard, disgusted at practice times:
    So it's your personal best
    Would it be impolite to . . .
    Hand the man his photos.
Upon their blocks
beside the washroom, dumb beside running water
poised as though to sip the narcissistic image, skim
new overlays, quaff the syrup water has dispersed –

beside adrenal timing, pineal switch, wire-released
photo-finish, no, not activated, hair-trigger
fingertip control/ is it/ sent the airborne evidence.
How will prints decipher
nor were treads
raised from the crime-scene:
   Cité Sportif,
the scrapbook of unpublished stats, the scrapbook
blows its paper discards across Sabra & Chatila.
Half-screen. For newsprint. High resolution mags.

   Upon their blocks

Get set

Scroll the channels

   Switch to surround

In their blanks they squat festooned in bling-bling,
envying wholeness, envying wholeness
recognised in total threat curled round a cider can,
the smart valise, pair of scissors, kindled aggro,
matronly disdain, how dare you third person me!
working out, working out
Personally ensconced in their living-rooms: this
is how life pans away, more or less alleviated,
lagged in the museum of childhood, staring

at vehemence, texting texting above the superbowl,
the shallow blood-filled saucer

Hang about
Hang about

CITÉ SPORTIF

Luminance. Slats intermitting despair in particles
voice here throat: resolve goes indigenous. Suppose
master of the ivory gavel beats
                    out irregularities,
musical wire & staves shunt a gated head-to-head
into a dream dwelling into the settlement again,
where are your winged outriders destined for,
the banks, the slats, the terraces, the rows?
        Cheered they may feel
        but by voices
        inlaid below, in ranks
        processed to appear
                paradise or suburb/
                explosion or pressure flask:
you do your best to disperse, they draw you back
in tar lumps, hooded, saying more than you ought,
the stadium power shorted, a cornered, trembling
appellate donned his body-pack, pulling to himself

himself he pitches one more sleight of redemption
face-on in a shadow-press of aides, spins lines
opposite to bulk the open shirt, the broad lapels,
    the bottler, the pressuriser
hauls back in turn,
coach guarantees condition once
led to the changing rooms, found fit, shot:

Cité Sportif.

Embedded in a leaf of slate he passes muster, door
slams behind then is sensed by an unfolding door.
On entry his chargecard was swiped,
    his charge sheet scanned.
Houris lounge across power-bumps.
          Receptionist
gesticulates at cool nurse conducting him across
to the cosmeticist. Departing the chair he slides
gold security card,
passport from a range.
    Nothing changes its in-
    scription, its in-numerals,
    its hologram,
    its beneath-the-lines.

A dining club door squelches back to let him pass.
　　The greeter glides forward assiduously.
The waiter flurries cloth, accepting him
from the far end, enticed into his personal chair
& re-embodied.
　　　　　　What
sherbet can I get you, purrs the sommelier,
since you betrayed your folks to get here,
what can I get you to feel, what performances,
what turns
　　do you bring to our party?
Dabbing at his mouth with starched napkin, dab-
bing at the spill on the table, blotting his investor's
dress-shirt, dabbing shit, body fluids, sir shall I
put this on your slate for you.

STEP BY STEP

Star-creases re-run themselves on the sky,
puckerings about knots of time lapsed
repeat; crows hang their murder bells
from time to time & in other branches.

Shamed figures taunted by implacable
cables of shine, shamed figures drift
with no comment, no reflection, each
clutches his or her open or unopened bag.

The patterns fall again, to same effect.
A blow in the face, a vicious thrust
learnt by accident carries on by ricochet.
Sustained in collapse the metal writhes,

windows fall in, their brilliant squares
land before the feet of the most damaged.
Stay with this language, hear its echo
over the years ring into a previous echo,

toe-taste a footfall into that acoustic
shame louvers, cables sing, the red tower
squats foundations, caves undervaults.
The grey escalator breaks, breaks, lifts

grey teeth biting through their comb shoe.

IPHIGENIA

A different line gives & takes & plays,
corded with lines of flight.
At outset
Out of errancy
lines of flight deviate from loaded flightpaths;
    & down a perplexed line,
some further line off our intended furrow
lags, resumes,
          detours ahead,
jerks & leaves its knots to hang in the air,
stratified cloud-cuckoo-land.
    Small wonder working upwards,
willing a definite line as though destined,
tied knots to play free,
          infinitely braiding,
    plans yet oppress the ground.

Cars snort openly & pull out.
Subways shudder, doors open. Dead names
crowd, carpet, stuff, upholster,
    piling it on thick
puffy quilted asphalt, napped concrete, trees
traumatised to mop-heads.
Wayward

bulk
encumbers the field.
                    A four-hour window
lag sickens,
lagging plugs the aperture, lint rises:
        stars decompensate & light breaks
a Western grant to be overrun
triple determines some thick curtaining
of ours,
                        hidden title,
        as pleating or laceration wouldn't.

Exact reflection blots out the original
A beam does not break but self-expunges
        Too much intensifier.
To be imperial hub
                    Come in, Come in,
multiplying, stuttering,
touches down with flocking copied escorts.
Stretch. Insert conduit.
Checksum.
Verify.
        Inaugurate a line of inquiry
blinds itself in childhood ullage, summons
Brillo Pads, Pritt-sticks,
        Brylcreem, mercury pomade,
The Popular Ford new-fledged.
                        Calculated smash.

Objects shorting overhead power-lines.
        Cavity wall wires

Whose loaded grid shocks tightly distances,
trailing through side-doors & traps,
          blockhouses, emplacements:
These cross-hatchings are its doing,
flipping open flaps, tiptoeing on brutal
    architecture,
finding spaces, winces.
      Considering the clip he goes,
basements rattle wide,
brother fortress
sticking out its siege of flying machines
         opens from within.
He sticks this for as long as viable.
             Walk & squawk.
Then he scrams in his new car
raising bright sleepless welts.

But the real work precedes such symptoms.
     Small wonder looking round –
           trailing edges,
paddles, slapping upwards like true selves
off the fattening surface –
smack each goes into the bulk drink,
    downed repeatedly,
    screw-tight,

shatter their own approach & first glimpses.
In cages in the basement
the illegals prepare food.

They conceal the turn, beyond the fast bends
or the slow bends, their blind turn granulates
economically, why the guardians are shutters!
light's held by them for congested objects
slotted between these boards: caparisoned
with beads of envy, stitches of dependency,
these are the most we have, our flicker book.

IPHIGENIA

You might untie a boat,

thereby slip down the lit
slipway into animate darkness,
waders drop from boltholes: down in the pit,
in the pen a hard silence,
    but this wind
through soughing willows has no remedy
it might turn to;
Haitian, Bangladeshi memories rock
treetops, floodplains can absorb no more
    habits of flesh,
      monsoons reach Montana,
        helicopters

faltering over their long-awaited patch.
They had been so long upheld
singly without knowing by these portions let
loose when designated:
    The deed applies to this grant only
    Inasmuch to risk the deed
aftermath
post hoc
the loaded phrase will have extended,
section files pressed into the deed as lines/
cordite puffs
between the outcrops
    so glum hardly worth
such slogging effort.
    Toll worth its deed, contumely,
              charge worth the phrase,
signalling clearance to our helicopters
sprout in their millions on salt pads,
raising dirt from every tuck,
raising dirt from every pocket.

    Simply put

this porcine para snarls at skinnies: Go! Go!
Fridges slosh suburban quarry tiles,
offloading their concealed

lit topslice from obese
earth, self-inculcated

Don't leave it capped.
A shaking hand brings a taper.

Push off, push into the spate

Peer out. The twin town, the flower
        The swollen race
                        Act now!
Slide down the bank softening,
dropped on the outskirts back of the rig,
chewing dirt
        The worst terrain
to vanish inside, you slam against a retaining
wall, a windbreak muscles up in thorns,
dikes impede you,
        testing fields grip ankles
Black earth, littered with brassica roots,
clumps bleeding feet
                        Voracious gulls.
Scabby earth thaws in thready light
infiltrating along its waterways.

The while maimed habit pulls the light cord,
shadows cast forward & backward
thickly off the hinges,
  old country's gangs
play on its foretellableness, bend
back with final snap repeating
lemon liqueur, mint tea,
blinis, betel. Filed
streamers, feathers gripped in the fist,
  cloud magnificence,
  visible signs made fixtures,
  gross vestige company –
  Be still,
lighten the panelled meadows, redeploy
the crabbed files to the outermost
wisps of presence –

  Compass-hauled I still
this near delinquent sky once I have sponged
expressions
off its slate,
    wiped off scribbles,
perversely slack
  traceries feebling faithfulness,
burning with split lip, chewing out stray
diligent paths & plans

wandering re-

capitulates, re-scores,

captures. Though I still

say, this is the place

spoken of & named, won't I still

clap the boards, report for my signing off,

clap the boards about a concrete bed.

Submitted flight-

plans having cleared

in bundles I shall enter them,

drill as though trepanning. Pastoral flutes

bore a thousand filaments.

Fasces.

Nazi occupied chateau.

Air smells as it did in the Alps,

vapour erases valleys.

No-mans-land abuzz

Command plus

Connect plus

Forward battery

pins me down in a defile, pounds into carbon

shies the ferny tracer,

reconciles at the hippocampus

errant halo

Larks, finches

choke their flight simulator, crash

feathery at the real threshold. Still

do what I expect of myself, still play turncoat.

Dutiful descant.

The material mind
won't weaken.
Events fall out just so.
The event shrinks from the necessary thought.
    Centre-stage but pluralling.

By pulling the cord I activate my manager,
          by this choice I hinge,
an elaborate structured emptiness
yawns heavily.
I have responded within 14 days,
I have responded,
    promptly claim my no-commitment
trial of a mute cookie.
The sentence is delayed hunger.
The rocks put on weight.
    Mud gets more muddy.
    Trails tangle & stiffen.

IPHIGENIA

They rigidify the airy squint, raise ocean
with their frothy blood, even the rocks swell
horrified, why the dead are not ghostly!
but contract to make more of flimsy projects.
We ply between economies: fixed rates
feed upon us & we feed on mucky fields,
our recompense the overabundance that presses.

Get on board now, get in, help up your father
on the gang-walk,
plenty bucks & welters below.
Twist one string so mother suffocates,
bandaged in enormous vestments.
        Or was it mother rolled
her corded sky-hanging of her own volition,
tropical print:

The wider-eyed her face, the heavier gauge
clouds a sky foregathering, one
overcast, one trashy-thatched,
loaded, hedge-trades to cover loss,
preoccupied with prospects for bottling plants,
        quick-assembled
        starter yeast, line operatives,
        interviewing temps, inter-agency –

slotted slickly in padded courts
fit for the sty's wallow, airy, rainy pellets,
                pasture preparing patties.
It's by such stockbreeding
cords play productively, a womb throws
bobbins into the tight courts,
into the padded breach:
        follow the storyline, delineate
the thread to where its hammock is swinging,

chase the story to a steroid pumped corpse
stripped & handsome,
surpassing use.
Chest-punctures bubble. Casting adjusts
snow flurries with the leaf plummets' tapping,
    bright flakes draw feeder lines,
    draw untangled harness,
small change through sorter trays
jiggles, stays in circulation, demands its cut,
spangled print.

For this will pay well. Confidants of the family,
    consiglieri
bulk out each to the ideal puff of vapour,
rolling through the sun's dip,
sip Krug, savouring Osetra
    watch field slaves
break aside in demurrage, lose the plot,
what complicates them? squatting on ankles,
time suspended rankles on their backs.

They defy the airy squint, curse the departed
from dehydrated mouths, the natural world un-
sockets from the social, god showing countenance
as though that would abash mastery. What?
A working day lengthens whatever is produced,
the ghosts of the dead drive machines
beautifully-engineered to collect the blood needed.

An unconditional line spools & wires
cross & at each junction with their wasted gifts
stand the resourceless:
failure is their set vocation, fail neatly, proof
not arrived-at but substantial in the frame
not entered but keyed,
        spiders them in stretch harness
propagates like knot-weed,
emphysema kelp.

IPHIGENIA

Visited on barley sugar barley water barley wine
        barley whoreson,
O barley cane John Barleycorn
Swollen in his coat he transubstantiates fume.
                    Lemon barley.
Whisky.
In this way the small grain gains bulk.

Starch fuels the floating factories'
        misbegetting
microphytic fronds hyper-propagate, block
any exit,
spiralling through vinegar,
thicken at the base of the alembic
        Thus too the surface creams & spumes.

Internal welts crimsoning, their congealed crime
        riveted each button door,
where yeast the human analogue, its cells'
limitations switching off, carcinogenic
floaters on Burgundy,
                performs wheelies, jack-knifes,
rides the premonition, rides before it curls
into cascade.

Every proposition swells, birthing clingy scarfs,
a jellyfish's lunar pulse.
The destroyers are fabulous too.
        I love the cars
        I love the cars
Whitening on the bench. The centrifuge.
The little fridge.
The strips of yeast cells as they stalk the earth.
        I love cigarettes.

Others snack on fattening rations, lifts rise
& plunge at one finger. Caged within music
they greet travellers, these our apparitions,
accruing light to us with retail cheer,
revel in such grocers' generosity, their con-
summate fervour. Using market movements
we invent new snacks for them, broker Fausts.

I like it sweet, I like it whipped, I like it salted,
             I like it fresh-churned.
Does the rose bush burnt from pure longing
        visited with fire rust,
transfigure in the blaze to the same figure?
The same shall furl & pack fire
into its prolific heads,
& does the blood-red garland
                    decked in thorns like spurs,

manifest the crowning dream of a virgin
wading through blood – Don't fuck with me:
I want the thick cultivar.
The sentence is delayed hunger.

IPHIGENIA

Shallow sphinx:
Untie the boat, launch with cloud-dwellers
rafts where lines finagle off-
handed, flick
        taunting
short of the air-grabbing hand,
lightning wanders & the moderate fasces
fall in general.
O you got green eyes o you got blue eyes O
        you got grey eyes
Flatten me too, confuse me.

At 7 a.m., hour of the smokers
Régie Turque, Passing Clouds
                    Rollup paper tears on the lip
on a bus out from Exeter,
yes you got hens teeth yes a blue moon/
        milk & honey.
Just like at 8 p.m. kids elbow past,
                    tastes
flap against the rocks & pools,
        Pickapeppa sauce on a barley fryup.
Clash City Rockers meet Deleuze '78
scenting moods like rooms,
scenting old rooms like moods,
roaming their slots.

Come the bath is salted.
Come the air fills with Ninjas.
Flatten knots into the limelight strings:
        Gossamer whips
leave off wrapping chrysalises.
Seeds hang in the cavities in the bath loofa,
                    swelling.
Yes every ventricle hides a new toy.
                The city
welters with blood when toys are seized.

Saddle meagre poleaxed.

Helicopters

stitch along the seams of a rifted

self-dormition, Parlophone, Tamla-Motown.

Shallow sphinx,

immune & free from all stain,

is it your whisper twists against my skin,

    each little status light blinking?

Snakes float in the muddy floodwater.

    I am eating too wildly

    I devour.

The dead too are sick from delayed hunger.

IPHIGENIA

Pitching or becalmed, head for that outcrop.

    Steadily she goes at hazard

shakes & cracks the slate

atlantic board & proving ground.

Sharp change of course, whose cant

a pilot reconciles,

    jockeying the chopper

through twin buttresses/ Hang on in

    High stakes players

vomit, slump on deck, drain power.

We played for the beheld sign

but dropped a bundle.

Terraform the asset earth on fractal outcrops.

A parsec would flood their outgoings. Crops
produce only indigestible trash,
         mortality is mocked
by lumps beneath each chair each papa
was ensconced on.
                  Open positions
fared poorly, picked off
data rummage, picked off squawk box,
         picked off instruction,
left marooned in the fateful bracket
swapping parts they need, stuck on outcrops.
Like so,

cutting each surmounter his slack. Scheduled
as his flight chases westward,
undercover agents & débridement
prepare a landing pad, doling
         sachet heaven –
harps in the countryside, simplicity,
paeans to the perfected thread.
Blood teems, a fixed thought
releases its myriad.
Over slow granite creep, out of exile,
         whirring eidetics
tilt into formation, flicker
mapped against these cloud-girded outcrops.

Queen of ships, chopper queen
Benign reaper,
                    Cast your reproving look,
reinstate history, free
wheels, lines, drawing out their implications.

Any throwing his foolish spool
chancily, snatching clothes
        draped with each morning,
plays directly to her hand shot out for fate's
        completer/finisher:

The thin rich
tread their uncoupled mills,
the sore poor children of some substance
shake shocked to eyes exposing them, behind
bust screens in trailers,
                    garb hurriedly:

Weight, cranked by much of less,
boosted competitively,
        toils choked water lapping
hurt amid serpents
dropped in sequence from the synaptic ledge,

credulous,
kneels to an obedient castle, it too tallies –
Before she snags the line in front
for a neck-tie, a vein-tie,
tussles to rise free of swelling, garrulous stone.

Queen of ships, in your praise she swells.
Queen of tumescent emptiness.

Home workers join in prayer at dusk, pins
bristle from tight mouths. Field servants
buckle-to; whose work, a watery surplus,
keeps body & soul together, but not theirs,
pre-dispensing any store they'd set aside –
While a smart enzyme from their trash,
traded on Chicago Futures, makes fortunes.

Chopper queen, lay the ground.
Scorched earth bloats.
Subsidiaries have hived off, clumped off,
chasing their profit,
revenants
shifting like the shadows overlap bellied urns.
Grease sapphire must be splurged
then the table drain,
the floor run like pulp pressing out paper,
trickle whey, grappa:
blot the malingerers, mop them up,
their fatty clouds can pile & drip with dawns,

they need the dawn but we distil,
they need bulk but we want cars.

Get back on board, spoilt, frisked & fevered.
Again the forebears plough ahead,
    cannibalised
in generous sweets, botox lips,
applying handles, thicken tongues.

Queen of angular heaven,
draw the line against these.

Benign reaper, all inherit.
Riffle out the deeds for this stake,
    they shall layer
like a reverse autopsy,
a back-handed archaeology restuffs the earth,
the puffy black & dark blue of poverty,
        thick soles.

They rigidify the airy squint, raise ocean
with their frothy blood, even the rocks swell
horrified, why the dead are not ghostly!
but the cellulite bulking out flimsy projects.
We ply between economies: fixed rates
feed upon us & we feed on mucky fields,
our recompense the overabundance that presses.

ORGANISE, MOVE AND BACK UP

Lines chair-lift their clutch of deep forest insects,
expropriating drops from humid air. Panoptic
creatures judged by a rangefinder, target cells
digitised in a block soup, draw down that fine-
beaded curtain, the curative darts, a lost tongue,
showing: *Only The Strong Survive, City of Ghosts*.
Now showing: the losses: gathered, irremediable.

Speculators float their up-country vision, piece
of action, ideal canopy-height perspective. Now
all earth's flocculence lies approved by yield,
sheaves pacify North Eastern hunting grounds.
The barbs of the ocean are drawn & justified,
insupportably dying in air. Steve, dinner. Friday,
switch cell account. Return DVD. Distinguish

Micronesian from Benin, peaceable tribes from
eaters of their fearless
      entrepreneurs of the new layer
sponsoring forest arts:
slit gong, eye slit, slit of the vulva, slit costume
             list & silt:

This potent object, this ritual object, this object
of unknown use,

     this slit object/
gash in a chilly envelope, gashes in a banner,
crucified body/
     into the midst of overplus
the ultimate floor-mix
     the multitudinous supper/
disclosure tears them apart, a disclosure troubles.
Blown out of the water. Depth-charge the dams.
The heavyweight tubers
jump up on the table,
     a load of opportunity
saturates the soil, saturates air, saturates water,
water to a breath-humid *fish-death! fish-death!*
     Boneless cemetery.

Glassy buoys jostle dead shoals, scant comfort
gapes for more. Scant cuts ease the opulent eye.
The eye coasts round the derrotero
     slitting parchment
              slitting vibrant blue.
Expectation gets one. The pageant hails one.
Available right now. An orchid, a monocarp/
forever & a day it blows.
Monotropa. Pale touch-me-not. The impatient.
Ghost flower. This is the last breeding pair.

Plied with birch bark & corn silk, infiltrators
might scrape by. Ghost kayakers had filched

yams, roasted them onshore, each spitting out
the tough bits, *Dogville, Mystic River.* Photo-op
gaze. Laugh off the alligator, grab a ragdoll,
profess to the okapi spirit, produce the phone.
The loss said soon mendacious, closes this slit

    listing, silted down.

ELEMENTARY FILM

after ABBAS KIAROSTAMI

So to test the water. Folded-wing hippogriffs
crowd the paved shadows, they'll be realised

lake from rill to shingle to humpback bridge
to this world, whose cinematic stiff, jewelled

assembly, scurrying through light, summoned,
signs undismayed. The courtesan's shadow

scuds & dragonflies, dragonflies float. Rain
clouds rub, overlapping overlapping, steered

confident when she glides to rendezvous, she
sings the while. It's raining, wakes nervous

hippogriffs who pawing the bridge in theory,
send their representatives, solid-hoofed

to break apart shadows, vein in spider glaze
lake from rill to shingle to humpback bridge,

veins of light lift a dragonfly. Light-trimmed
her stiff, jewelled ruffles had been fingered

& thought soft: the world keeps a distance,
disappointed, this world says so little, slough

a little inflates, furls its several consequences
into the hideyholes, bright pockets stitched

to a landscape clearly planted in all senses.
These are odd creases, much as I'd thought,

says she, it's chance the wrinkles of avoiding
should like this repeat the wrinkles of meeting.
    Chance indeed:

        Best thing were
lurch stunned on their glittering footplates,
shining bridge cables
        stunned here to drift
without response or proposition, turn ugly
witnessing a street assault, a transferred
        package, angry at un-
        reasonable distress,
where the fired body remains intact yet still
unknowably damaged,
                or if known unfelt:

Best thing to pad through shattering puddles,
        safe in a carbonised

     wire tunnel, anti-
vandal paint, flash bounces back from a hurt,
makes glass opaque,
     F-16 hippogriffs
fly off to Ireland, Nubia or Cyprus
               bearing others' markings:

once these furlings have unfurled, rolled back
shadows superimposed to show a causeway

creep like eventide beckons, lays on thick
lake from rill to shingle to humpback bridge,

horses of instruction are recalled to the stables,
leaving the field to monsters. Light delegates

fleet of foot, the outriders to flies' agitation,
tangle with black candlewick, intrusive twigs,

imperative softening. These serried courtesans
break towards their summoners, they flutter

not so much skin-deep as a translucent body
showing its inner shadows' assembly. Rented

pockets alive, every grab-bag seething. None
says she, I'd be content to loiter, deep scale. I

see my convolutions layer, a slapped surface
                coinage/
    light skint/
what do I have to do
    with such invitation
soon clears up. She's shouldering her satchel,

forward feet, shadows snatching at her fiercely,
lake from rill to shingle to humpback bridge.

MARRAM SCAFFOLD

following BARBARA GUEST

Climb the sand horn, the aspirated engine does.
Salts darken in the day's advance.

What unearthly reeled back
designed to withstand, with its big warm opulence

attracted swimmers. Hence the cove
colour pencil. A choir diminishes in wavelets

floppy garlands paddle. The wash is what piles up
against a construction site,

swept that mudbank clear as mud,
dissonant for fear of dissonance. Trembling air dies

or does the one stood at once transformative.
You must undergo. As does fragile,

as dies the pinafore as gaping flies,
instances I'd weathered & whose molten ordnance

jumped but without aspiring, but then jump
might no more than drop. Darkening lights,

a sickle falls & visible monuments
stand up to their knees, prurient groping, a wrong

headed scrabble under the revealed lid,
measures dunes refaced for masquerade, like the

bolted heads below the cube, an engineer
mouth taped in the shadow of a smashed aqueduct.

Believe sand. Convince sand.
The absorbed woman takes down the curtain,

twilight presses on these deserts she has cornered.

DOWN TO EARTH:
A REDACTION

Of its greatness the sun sups of gasoline,
smacking forecourts, licking hearts
lubed with sealed-in blood — break them
methodically, remove while they yet pump,

for each component's certain to outdo
more cautious visions, to exceed or floor
graphs by actuaries: out crawl carers
surreptitiously, welling from their open pit.

Residues flare in asphalt pools, volatiles
spill in parking lots where overheated
agents poke beneath hoods, throw
keys to a collector. They sweat copiously

but let the hearts twitch, pay their dues
then walk, they know how. A flight of birds
ignites against a sunset, blackening
in short order. Of its greatness the sun

asks more to burn, yet more to evaporate:
obedient, oh no wobbling, carers set to,
filling quotas in an immolation park,
smirking by the lines. The sinking fund,

shale library, compress to utmost drops.
Canadian sands crush; heart's pre-emptive
impulses crush too. Thumps consummate,
not a baton's tap. Not the thump at its

life's own pace, no the thumping wakes
votaries to greatness. A snatch, a skip, as
if it rang out true time, as if their crisp
snare were damped, dicrotic but reliable,

sending children forth in bubble-wrap,
alert to metre, calm with methylphenidate.
Organs shall be chained so then output
more effectively. Tuned to work with

willing clouds, willing currents, willing
followers whose mode, touch, hints,
time-keepers constant to their rooted beat,
through transcription move in phalanxes,

delivered by the skip-full only, skips
abundant in this free scrapyard. Just
put everything into the skip, no overheads
trouble offshore derricks when they nod

like a lossless engine in its anaerobic
chamber, turning at a distance, transmutes
nothing into fresh air, field staff report,
overawed. This nothing cranks its shaft,

encrypting data for shell companies,
masking ownership; it comes up in roses,
wafts light & heat with gently-beating
stamina. Should ever timing-chain snag

its unmetaphysical hook, sheer away cogs
shunting children down; sparse gusts of
vapour pegged between stars, will spell
a name suppressed, a child's breath

suspended on the negative, will imprint
the shadow of the cloud morning burnt off.
Tracing invisible writing, sexual spill
slathers grass, gas notates a blind gut,

but a blade shaves earth like cheek or table,
wipes the contract. Could ever air's writ
attract Melaina to the forecourt left
dark for her form, heart she made pound.

Δ

The sun of its greatness would restrict
movement. The sun of its nearsightedness
gets in close & licks the face it pillages
for next course. Proud sun's reserve

army of space-heaters now will field its
Mexicans & Poles, they turn up or dig into
what rainfall or cash-in-hand permit,
lifting tubers in their scant down-time,

who reap some wetted richness by day
turn their hands, turn then to improvise
with shucks of shade against gullies,
tucked inside clefts, hideout near a river.

Behind rubbish bins, fuel distributors
trade their chips of sunlight, gilded
child oblation fuels this energy exchange
in lorry-loads, children at a high point

of blood-standing, all of most, most
reckoned, most admired, irreplaceable,
of soft-pillowed, all most precocious
in astronomy, forever pitched in to scythe —

these gas-holders, fume-breathers, fume-
exhalers sprint round the ball-court
throwing shapes at each other, aching
to feed furnaces, get sent up in smoke:

Corn-reefs half-protect the quiver-nerved
brat who scarpers, neat dodger, gold-
spotted, burnt, dapple-limned ocelot
head-butts a lading gate & fuel tanks,

panting with tongue lolling, edging over
sandy ground, wriggles beneath radar
on his stomach, sand burns & wafts
recompense to heaven; heaven that exacts

life for life, accepts the surplus & spoils,
snorting incense up from furnaces,
the subtilised, the fluted shearing
inwardness of later wreathing substances,

blue gas futurity, stirred up in tornadoes,
cyclones of furious disbursement, kids
tugged off to lymph camps, ripping
down a tidemark's tar & toil, throatily

to sear, drown, clench. Powered by such
zeal, how could they fail to provide,
pressed hard, spun dry, collectors mass
like cotton what children had yielded.

Tide them over. Where blacktop unrolls,
grunt cars. Hear that votive prattle grate.
Car prototypes wink on Mayan floors,
soak up whatever, slopping like a low-

consumption valve, processing the ghost
files, children cupping cheaper gas.
A totem pole resplendent playing out
its bindings of copper. The smirking head

expresses tears. What runs dependably
has its effect, engines flew across parks
from car bombs, scattered shrieks behind;
now newly innocent smiles readjust,

crushed envisaged blessings surge,
sun whose garish splash, yolk calendars,
destroys all hearts, prises open walls
of milk, of blood, oil, rods & concrete.

Δ

Crept from degraded bags, sputtered out of pipes
in soaking bulges spiky roots, warms bolts, frost-
frees the fused plates, ejecting plugs of glacial ice,

aligns them though at odds, ironing out divisions I
for one thought everlasting. Succumb to warmth,
passively disposed because of sun's people, smart

couples, clusters, singletons, affable communities,
each has a lodging place, buys or sells a footprint,
nestled in the shadow of a red rock or green hand.

The layers are sanded sheer, their linen naps tight,
curves take the wheel & the hinterland is promise
past reproof, fortunately no stations, merely stops,

though cats-eyes pop, bridges warp, levees break,
aggressive grilles forge deep welts down four-lane
furrows boiling rivers discharge into, primping up

prairie grass the aimed tornadoes flattened, scythe
mohican cuts, buffalo waves, & gap-tooth railings
crumple: blood-stained rocks, green-bespattered,

lurch & sway alongside, washed from earthworks,
meteors they may be, lumpy vectors splatting life:
is this the best evidence on waking they peel back

their carbon copies to parade? left but the leavings,
labyrinthine trash-pickers find their trash swiped
in trades for new apartments. Mutually dependent

cone sections buried like a dog its bone, prescient
or come to that, produced as if hatched out today,
touched up, licked a little, set in favourable light;

surface never takes the pigment, nor Sue or Katie,
any employee, risks indelible love but so defaced,
which means a comprador must grease his way in

patriotic slogans, teams & bands, the Alleghenies,
heat-bonded overlays machined to shrug pliantly,
to warp in time while owning to but too solid earth,

though smart cones pour out sunlight, furring up
on transcendental poles; presently footage shows
confused drivers age on leaf-fall, overshoot ramps,

these for solos, these for armoured convoys, these
plausibly, were colander for cress, go for saplings
hell-for-leather, since its highs look down on them,

go for stumps ruffed in beefsteak fungus, up from
thoughtful earth the map of undertakings, surface
ghosts whose subterranean bodies fling out spores

since their depths look plausibly like height put on,
how say you blind in scurf, would wrinkled sleeve
puff up like gelatine, a blue January atmosphere

the night's flats distend & fill with stormy flickers,
pavement quilts, blacktop bulges, & its presences
wreathe inky pumice in fine spray or steam wisps.

That was the future, backing deep into a thick sky
as the securely gated, as the reassuringly patrolled
play at corralling steers & heating branding irons.

Δ

Until it stiffed we ran our car heater, burning first
the spare then all the car tires for warmth, Miguel
went for help but had not eaten, so without a hat—

Sue or Kate I doubt. Ramon, José, play their slots,
their slots the chance all take, their slots the altar,
lights ablaze, chrome-crusted, radiant in clearings

spread a make-shift stall, from staging areas post
bites on lunar chafing trays, tuck hors d'oeuvres
in king beds whose perturbations flex; but border

vigilantes drawing on their babies with a flourish,
chalk or lead, blast holes behind an altar triptych,
fucked angelic spirits blip & scuffle truly headless

chickens, o the heck we are, flitting flattened soil
plunge in gullies, crest a foaming ridge, headfirst
dive at straining cars, wriggle into T & pants, tire-

scorch a bottle clearing, grubbing up an underlay
deposited in panic, strike the tents, gather kids,
gun for breakneck cortège. A caravan of fugitives

hotrods its tanks of bio-fuel towards high tunnels
ripening these tulips & tomatoes, the pick of each
graded through the shuttle combs where business

plays out fiercely, bison trains, fenders slamming
obstacles aside, the windshield splatted galaxies
obliterated, buffalo's de luxe trim smashing trees,

now why relinquish such minnow stuff I'd earned
but best invest it in that shadow trust, delivering
returns a thousand-fold from our stake, originals

spread-eagled on the hoods are beasts & children,
ice collects from bloody nostrils, any agent going
sacrificed to bring on roses, distant polypropylene

scoops the productivity from ice-glaze in its plates
propped on edge, across the sky the bees & moths
scrawl the life sentence, cosmic excise hoovers up

dust due. Would its depth-effect enhance on low-
glare panels, feel warmer, much as though insides
palpated, touched through valued sky were gently

slashed with that mare's-tale switch their searches
like a comet's tail drawl? Wheat struts in reap-me
phalanxes, oceans combing down deranged locks

settle into corn-rows, settle in a fish-tank striation,
so lines are laid, but plasma ghosts show through,
insides circulate like burps & farts warm the shed

behind the true solar panel, feed-back sky stapled
perfectly, not one pocket, not one slot, the finest
membrane lets go showers of perspiration in veils:

damp joggers kick into the drift of epithelial cells,
loop skid-marks, etch blinding furrows with their
burning glasses, superficial drapes, prototypes of

more fields, electronic prairies, page paging page.
There will be work. There will be school. Rammed
along its folds, the bedroll underpins the landscape.

Δ

Whose beauty is deposited on drenched
lawns by solar edict, daubed over roofs
between the aerials & dishes, sluiced
yellow leukocytes on walls? Some defer to

the beauty of outputs, while indirection
casts a more gentle spell. The source
primeval lavishes the balm it scarfs up,
bestows gouts of insatiable consumption.

Clouds venture forth as silver rocks
float across a trading-floor. No beyond
advanced from the distant circle, only
boulders bob like buoys at the perimeter:

self-consuming can't restore that rift
by putting out. From rubble burying a car
they will stagger, toting glass vessels
drooped from the eye to tease the press,

& where the moon shifts, ganders off,
spills burn into car hoods, & under seats
propane cylinders with heat jackets
wait for the phone to chirp, children

dance before the call connects, the sonne
schedules its fix of unalterable truth
scoring welts over armadillo backs
prostrate in work & in worship. Daily

rituals of the canyon, ledged adolescents,
lubricate the dry spring. Much-favoured
lips pout before their idols, packet
fire glams their every orifice as moist,

& a prepared offspring will be their surety
prospected in the blocks. Hypocrisy
bonds the prayerful with hedonists,
shifting goods like down a sushi track,

smashing through rubble for its wafer lode
of credit, goods in heaven, goods on tick
flap through rafters of the trading floor
drawing fire, then will doves descend

in a goblin market, show their hearts
to day workers; claiming kind for kind
they pluck out stones, for this is rapturous
energy transfer at work. Airlanes conduct

to LA, barrios will air-condition Texas,
try-outs glamourous as Mixcoatl
leave their ball court for the antechamber,
shaping up for sacrifice with sun's chop.

I hear them call from every skip, I hear
them when I skip a beat, the beat is theirs,
the thump against the basket, the basket
calcifying, arteries are hardening like

coral, hear them moan in compaction
machines, hear the hiss from valves
in the soil of the brownfield site; & in skips
charged with rubble, intervals of throat

clutch, the intervals of palate strop, the
full skips of the disregarded, scarcely
noticed, lunar run-off shines like mercury.
Balloons float in a shrine in Pittsburgh.

Δ

Great is Artemis. Her temple will be lead-shielded,
purlieus sealed in UN safekeeping, permanently.

Seal the hot springs & ice over the distinctive rills.
Their spoilage will compress into bars & blocks,

smooth tablets marked with component time-code,
heat must be contained, leaching of excess water

spun off from expressways & steeply-raked fields.
What's buried never rots. The dead cavort on film,

prancing down the beach before the consistorial
elders, they'll milk them like they're plump aphids,

they'll drink anything to stay active, laugh at death
when jilted again by heartthrobs as the reel turns:

Great is Artemis. She feeds us our compensation,
spilling silverly in furrows. But her temple is shot,

clad within its concrete Parnassus. Games persist,
the velvet stage trots out Lipizzaner miniatures

& toy poodles. One more encore shouldn't harm.
Return these to the video vault, tick box for Billie

Holliday, request the Leontyne Price, take out the
grandparents, take out Emmett Till, temperature-

assured to never die, subsist in chains of zeroes
countermanding the deep chain of one, Artemis:

ritualistic stoning, nooses drop, clouds disperse
cold triggers over peach groves, breadbaskets etc..

Great is Artemis. Her life is squander, her people
work their butts hard to rankle her riddled flumes.

Her most militant snorkelled off Phuket. Bar-girls
turn tricks before chamber mouths & love-bomb,

servants of the bitch of Ephasus. Great is Artemis.
She takes fierce bends on mountains on her 650,

she holes up deep below the finances, disburses
through the vents & cubby-holes, risks life & limb

to prostitute herself, she has spread herself across
the *temenos*, across the piste, she extracts what-

ever lucre these moneymen might still lay on her,
gobbling the jackpot, sliding, ribboning the Alps.

Great is Artemis. Springtide dribbles through the
egg flint embankments, rills along their ditches.

Bond issue oozes out of silos, pours into valleys
waste disposal companies strew with wide limbs

she loves to see root-confused, it's her advantage
played by gulls & traders swooping at the plough,

cattle egrets blown off-course, wrappers chucked
from roundabouts, buckets-full of chicken wings

comply before the off. Accumulation's demigods
stand dignified while strafed on blaring podiums.

Lenses bulge. Many of them bogus, went direct
from id to item, still their fear conforms the lanes,

fear of the non-recording angel, violent vacancy,
so all stuff themselves, no crack or gap or mouth,

that's great. Then we thaw. For great is Artemis
who never watches, never looks in wing-mirrors.

They are the road's curves that steer my car. Tatty
triangles of grass alongside interchanges, serve

notice, serve her through a dot matrix, rampant
rusty prophetesses stretch arms studded red with

nourishment or pain's swellings, lumps flare up,
fizzle big with heat. Milk them. Great is Artemis.

www.ingramcontent.com/pod-product-compliance
Lightning Source LLC
Chambersburg PA
CBHW031126090426
42738CB00008B/991